2nd Book of Devotionals

John "Cleve" Stafford

Published by John "Cleve" Stafford, 2024.

While all precautions have been taken in the preparation of this book, the publisher assumes no responsibility for errors, omissions, or damages resulting from the use of the information contained herein.

2nd BOOK OF DEVOTIONALS

First edition. February 24, 2024.

Copyright © 2024 John "Cleve" Stafford.

ISBN: 979-8-9900544-3-1

Written by John "Cleve" Stafford.

Table of Contents

Chapter 1 | The Armor of God 1
Chapter 2 | Watch Your Language; He Is Listening 4
Chapter 3 | Calming Your Stormy Seas 6
Chapter 4 | The Real Hero of the Story 8
Chapter 5 | Faithful Thomas 10
Chapter 6 | Walking on Water 13
Chapter 7 | The "Mystery" 15
Chapter 8 | Mother's Day Should Be Every Day 18
Chapter 9 | Finish Your Spiritual Race 21
Chapter 10 | The False Promise on the Mountain 23
Chapter 11 | Don't Join Them in the Dark 25
Chapter 12 | Will the Real Noah Please Stand 27
Chapter 13 | The Attack Against Christianity 29
Chapter 14 | Will You "Pay It Forward?" 31
Chapter 15 | The Temptations of Jesus 33
Chapter 16 | Happy Marriage (pt. 1) 35
Chapter 17 | Happy Marriage (pt. 2) 37
Chapter 18 | Happy Marriage (pt. 3) 39
Chapter 19 | Happy Marriage (pt. 4) 41
Chapter 20 | No "Made by God" Sticker 43
Chapter 21 | To Believe or Disbelieve 45
Chapter 22 | Why Do We Sing in Church? 47
Chapter 23 | Repentance Is Not Optional 49
Chapter 24 | Keep the Knots Securely Fastened 51
Chapter 25 | By No Means the Least 53
Chapter 26 | Types of Confession in the NT 55
Chapter 27 | Rushing to Their Demise 57
Chapter 28 | Spare Them a Thought and a Prayer 59
Chapter 29 | Psalms 23 (pt. 1) 62
Chapter 30 | Psalm 23 (pt. 2) 64
Chapter 31 | Psalm 23 (pt. 3) 67
Chapter 32 | Psalms 23 (pt. 4) 69
Chapter 33 | Psalms 23 (pt. 5) 71

Chapter 34 | Psalms 23 (pt. 6) 73
Chapter 35 | Psalms 23 (pt. 7) 76
Chapter 36 | Psalms 23 (pt. 8) 78
Chapter 37 | Psalms 23 (pt. 9) 81
Chapter 38 | Move On or Feel and Stop? 84
Chapter 39 | Hold Fast to the Traditions 86
Chapter 40 | Don't Raise a "Monster" 88
Chapter 41 | No Longer the Moral Compass 90
Chapter 42 | The Old vs. The New 93
Chapter 43 | Beatitude (pt. 1) The Poor in Spirit 95
Chapter 44 | Beatitudes (pt. 2) The Poor in Spirit 97
Chapter 45 | Beatitudes (pt. 3) Those Who Mourn 99
Chapter 46 | Beatitudes (pt. 4) The Meek 101
Chapter 47 | Beatitudes (pt. 5) Hunger and Thirst 103
Chapter 48 | Beatitudes (pt. 6) The Merciful 105
Chapter 49 | Beatitude (pt. 7) The Pure in Heart 107
Chapter 50 | Beatitudes (pt. 8) The Peacemakers 109
Chapter 51 | Beatitudes (pt. 9) Persecuted 111
Chapter 52 | What Does Your Heart Reflect? 114
Chapter 53 | Last, Most Desperate Thing We Do 116
Chapter 54 | Fruit of the Spirit (pt. 1) Love 118
Chapter 55 | Fruit of the Spirit (pt. 2) Joy 121
Chapter 56 | Fruit of the Spirit (pt. 3) Peace 123
Chapter 57 | Fruit of the Spirit (pt. 4) Patience 125
Chapter 58 | Fruit of the Spirit (pt. 5) Kindness 127
Chapter 59 | Fruit of the Spirit (pt. 6) Goodness 129
Chapter 60 | Fruit of the Spirit (pt. 7) Faithfulness 131
Chapter 61 | Fruit of the Spirit (pt. 8) Gentleness 133
Chapter 62 | Fruit of the Spirit (pt. 9) Self-control 135
Chapter 63 | Preach the Word of God, not Man 137
Chapter 64 | Be Careful of a Large Hammer 139
Chapter 65 | Instant Gratification = Eternal Regret 141
Chapter 66 | Which One Are You? 143
Chapter 67 | The Power of His Whisper 145
Chapter 68 | Religious Freedom? 147

Chapter 69 | What Do You Think Your Soul Is Worth?........................ 149
Chapter 70 | He Is Waiting to Hear from You 151
Chapter 71 | Who Is Your Focus?.. 153
Chapter 72 | Don't Squander God's Gifts 155
Chapter 73 | The Dangers of Being Unequally Yoked 157
Chapter 74 | Pay no Attention to Them 159
Chapter 75 | Wisdom over Health, Wealth, and Power....................... 161
Chapter 76 | Be Subject to the Governing Authorities 163
Chapter 77 | At the Bottom of the Ocean 166
Chapter 78 | Thank You, God, Thank You, Jesus..................................... 168
Chapter 79 | Correcting an Opponent with Gentleness..................... 170
Chapter 80 | Deny, Carry, Follow 173
Chapter 81 | The Resurrection Was No Hoax 175
Chapter 82 | My First and Foremost Love 177
Chapter 83 | Continue in What You Have Learned.............................. 179
Chapter 84 | Like a Superhero but More Powerful 182
Chapter 85 | Encouraged Today, Doomed Tomorrow........................ 184
Chapter 86 | Church Leaders Don't Own You 187
Chapter 87 | Just.Don't.Give.Up. 189
Chapter 88 | When God Calls... 191
Chapter 89 | The Secret Message on Your Tombstone 193
Chapter 90 | Encourage Future Preachers.. 195
Chapter 91 | Becoming a More Effective Proclaimer 197
Chapter 92 | The One Who "Shuts the Doors?"....................................... 200
Chapter 93 | What Will Your Response Be? 203
Chapter 94 | From God's Word, Not Man's Books 206
Chapter 95 | Step Out of the City 209
Chapter 96 | She Is More Than I Deserve 212
Chapter 97 | Courage Under Fire 214
Chapter 98 | Clarity From a Missing Verse 216
Chapter 99 | The Challenge to Dig Deeper 218
Chapter 100 | There Is Strength in Numbers 220

Foreword

The second set of 100 daily articles was written a year after the first and, like the first set, was not arranged in any specific chronological order. Most articles were written in response to local or global events and people's concerns; some were simply my reflections on various topics. Again, I want to thank everyone who encouraged me to write and publish these articles, including Cathy, who responds to them almost daily and isn't shy about pointing out any mistakes.

A special note to my sister, Coleen, whom I was fortunate enough to baptize in November 2024. It has been three months since that day, and I could not be prouder of her commitment. She memorizes scriptures daily, studies, attends church regularly, and prays all the time. Since I live across the ocean, she is also "in charge" of spreading the true "Good News" to family members. Love you, big sis.

I must also mention my two granddaughters, the Butterfly and Unicorn Princesses, who inspire me to be better every day. The Butterfly Princess always wants the first copy of every book, and naturally, she gets it. They also have an Easter egg in every book I publish. Lastly, I want to recognize all my Christian friends who encourage me by reading these articles daily and are unafraid to correct me. We all need accountability partners, and they certainly fulfill that role in my life.

Of course, my beautiful and devoted Christian wife, Melinda, is foremost among those who inspire and encourage me. She has steadfastly supported me and is a pillar in the work at the church. Mel, always and forever, my love.

PS. People have noticed that I always capitalize "Him" or "He" when referring to God and Jesus. The scripture quotes do it differently, but I can't write them in lowercase—it's just my thing.

Chapter 1
The Armor of God

"Finally, be strong in the Lord and in the strength of his might" (**Eph. 6:10**). Being a Christian is tough; it can feel daunting and overwhelming to others, which might lead them to react negatively. It seems as if we are constantly under attack, and for good reason – we always are. The devil desires your soul and will use all his considerable power to separate you from the love, mercy, and protection of God. To achieve this goal, he will manipulate those closest to you, tempt you with the allure of material possessions, and bring illness and financial struggles upon you and those you love. He will also employ envy, jealousy, doubt, and temptation to potentially make you stumble.

Nothing gives him more joy than seeing another soul forever lost to darkness, and he is relentless and ruthless in his pursuit of it. The good news is that you are not alone. God promises that He will always be on your side. The author of **Heb. 13:5** reminds us of this with the words, "...for He has said, "I will never leave you nor forsake you." It should be comforting and encouraging to know that during those times when you are enduring what seems to be unbearable challenges. However, we have more than just His promise to walk beside us during difficult times—He also provides us with everything we need for the battle. **Eph. 6:11** reminds us to "Put on the whole armor of God so that you may be able to stand against the schemes of the devil."

That's right; we have a complete set of armor to protect us from the wily ways of Satan. We are given all the necessary tools to ensure our victory against him. God's strength is without equal, and the devil is a vanquished foe before he even launches his first attack, but we must never underestimate his power. **Eph. 6:12**,

> "For we do not wrestle against flesh and blood, but against the rulers, against the authorities, against the cosmic powers over this present darkness, against the spiritual forces of evil in the heavenly places."

Do not be deceived; the enemy is a powerful adversary capable of inflicting much harm and anguish, but fear not and never retreat. He has all the weapons of the world on his side. He will send enemies dressed as friends and will appear to have your back. Those "friends" will gain your confidence and slowly try to lure you away from God's protection. At other times, the attack will be as ferocious as you can imagine – the sudden ailing health or the tragic loss of a loved one so precious to you that life without them will seem hopeless.

Don't wait for that to happen before reaching for your armor. If you do, the fight will seem hopeless, and your embattled, broken spirit will have to fight in a weakened state. But know that even then, victory is assured. Do what **Eph. 6:13-17** tells you to do,

> "Therefore take up the whole armor of God, that you may be able to withstand in the evil day, and having done all, to stand firm. Stand therefore, having fastened on the belt of truth, and having put on the breastplate of righteousness, and, as shoes for your feet, having put on the readiness given by the gospel of peace. In all circumstances take up the shield of faith, with which you can extinguish all the flaming darts of the evil one; and take the helmet of salvation, and the sword of the Spirit, which is the word of God."

This does not mean that battles will be lost, that scars won't accumulate along the way, or that the enemy won't gain ground from time to time – this is the nature of warfare. However, it means that the right attitude and obedience to the One who strengthens you assures you of final victory. Learn from the temporary losses, fortify your spiritual armor, and study the Word to increase the power of your defenses. And do not hesitate to go on the attack. Cast aside the devil and his plans with your knowledge of the Word and steadfast faith in the Almighty, omnipotent, and invincible God of creation.

And remember, pray, pray, pray. It is your most effective tool because communication with the commander God will undoubtedly ensure victory. Persevere when all seems hopeless, get back up when knocked down, fight back with all your might, and take comfort in knowing God is fighting alongside you. **Jos. 1:9**,

> "Have I not commanded you? Be strong and courageous. Do not be frightened, and do not be dismayed, for the Lord your God is with you wherever you go."

Chapter 2
Watch Your Language; He Is Listening

I want to begin this article with a warning and an apology: a warning because it includes two commonly used partial acronyms that use God's name in vain, and an apology for using them in the context of the article. **Col. 3:8**, "But now you must put them all away: anger, wrath, malice, slander, and obscene talk from your mouth." In his letter to the Colossian church, Paul had a lot to say that is relevant to us, and today, I want to focus on the phrase, "...obscene talk from your mouth." Over time, our language has descended into what can only be described as precariously awful. "Awful" because of the language used, and "precarious" because of where it leads the speaker.

Let's begin with what I consider the vilest of all obscene talk. In **Exo. 20:7**, we read, "You shall not take the name of the Lord your God in vain, for the Lord will not hold him guiltless who takes his name in vain." The worst ugliness that comes from people's mouths, including many Christians, is expressly forbidden in the Ten Commandments. Nowadays, it seems nearly impossible to watch a movie or a television show without hearing the term "om...!" However, that isn't the only term used; another is "J...C...!" While the former is more commonly heard, both are equally blasphemous and must be avoided at all costs.

The saddest thing about this is that their prevalence in almost every aspect of life, including entertainment, politics, and everyday speech, has caused many Christians to be guilty of using them. I often say to my wife that it sounds like an American motto and is used to express happiness, sadness, excitement, and disgust. Is it mocking God, though? Yes, even if the speaker is unaware, which is highly doubtful if they are a Christian. There is a warning in the Bible about mocking God that should be carefully read and kept in the forefront of every mind. **Gal. 6:7**, "Do not be deceived: God is not mocked, for whatever one sows, that will he also reap."

We should never fall into the trap of thinking that words "don't matter" if they are not explicitly meant. Moreover, what does it say about Christianity if non-believers hear the supposed children of God blaspheme the One they claim to revere and follow? Other curse words, disparaging phrases, and lewd language have become so common that they no longer seem to raise an eyebrow among many Christians. Personally, I believe that a lack of proper vocabulary compels the speaker to use foul language to convey their point. It is also intentionally used to intimidate or provoke someone, often leading to arguments and fights. **Eph. 5:4**, "Let there be no filthiness nor foolish talk nor crude joking, which are out of place, but instead let there be thanksgiving."

We should never engage in anything that brings disgrace to ourselves or our God. It's important to clearly communicate to others that we do not want to hear foul language from them. The issue is that many hesitate to do so because they fear losing a "friend" more than they fear the consequences of their actions. As a result, they either ignore the behavior or pretend they didn't hear it. Years ago, a young girl in our church exemplified what a Christian should be in this regard. She was a teenager in high school at the time, but she showed no fear in admonishing those who used foul language around her. When I asked her if she was scared of their reaction, she replied, "No, I don't need friends who act that way."

What a lesson for all of us. Why wouldn't we stand up for morally sound speech, and why wouldn't we admonish those who use our Father's name in vain? But above all, why would we blaspheme the name of God, who gave His Son as a sacrifice to allow us to have the hope of a place in heaven? Watch your language because He is listening.

Chapter 3
Calming Your Stormy Seas

> "And when he got into the boat, his disciples followed him. And behold, there arose a great storm on the sea, so that the boat was being swamped by the waves; but he was asleep. And they went and woke him, saying, "Save us, Lord; we are perishing. "And he said to them, "Why are you afraid, O you of little faith?" Then he rose and rebuked the winds and the sea, and there was a great calm. And the men marveled, saying, "What sort of man is this, that even winds and sea obey him?" (**Mat. 8:23-27**).

What a strange question to be asked by the disciples who had witnessed miracles performed by Jesus: "What sort of man is this?...," The answer should be evident to any Christian. The Son of God is the only "man" who could rebuke a storm. That miraculous act would have convinced me rather than placed a seed of doubt in my mind. Witnessing such power over the forces of nature would have solidified His deity for me. The same Jesus who said in **Joh. 8:58**, "Truly, truly, I say to you, before Abraham was, I am," could also walk on water, raise the dead, expel demons, restore sight to the blind, and make a crippled person dance.

He could also provide more fish than a net can hold, turn water into wine, and restore an opponent's ear, so I am confident that calming a stormy sea was well within His power. We do not praise a savior limited in His power but one "through whom all things were created." In **Mat. 28:18**, we read that "all authority in heaven and on earth" was given to Him, so it stands to reason that He has authority over the forces of nature as well. And since He is, in essence, God, here is what He is capable of: **Job 38:4-11**,

> "Where were you when I laid the foundation of the earth? Tell me, if you have understanding. Who determined its measurements—surely you know! Or who stretched the line upon it? On what were its bases sunk, or who laid its cornerstone, when the morning stars sang together and all the sons of God

shouted for joy? Or who shut in the sea with doors when it burst out from the womb, when I made clouds its garment and thick darkness its swaddling band, and prescribed limits for it and set bars and doors, and said, 'Thus far shall you come, and no farther, and here shall your proud waves be stayed?"

Those words spoken to Job illustrate His limitless power, and if it is His, then it also belongs to His Sons. How awesome is it that we worship a God who created every subatomic particle that makes up every atom in the entire universe? The point of all the explanations above is this: If Jesus can do all those seemingly impossible things, He can also calm our storms. They may arise rapidly and be devastating, threatening to drown us in an ocean of pain and anguish. So we cry out to Jesus, "Save us!" We claim to know Him and have unwavering faith, but when the storm rises to test our faith, we panic and cry out for help instead of standing firm.

Then, Jesus can say the same thing He said to His disciples: "Why are you afraid, O you of little faith?" However, the real beauty of the story is that even as He questions our faith, He speaks the words to calm the storm. You see, His love for us is so strong that He willingly sacrificed His Son for our promise of a better future, so it stands to reason that He would do anything for us. This does not mean storms will not arise, but it does mean our faith will call Him into action on our behalf. So, if you are in the midst of a storm and crying out to Him, know that He hears you and will save you. Maybe not exactly how you expect or even understand right now, but in a way that aligns with His will.

Chapter 4
The Real Hero of the Story

"In the beginning was the Word, and the Word was with God, and the Word was God. He was in the beginning with God. All things were made through him, and without him was not anything made that was made" (**Joh. 1:1**).

If I asked you to tell me about your favorite hero in a story or movie, would you be able to do so? Most people would jump at the chance and spend as much time as I would allow, regaling me with story after story of their hero or heroine's exploits. If I were to ask you to tell me about all the other characters, would you be able to do that as well? Once again, most people I've spoken with can recall so much about mostly fictitious characters in movies that I am left in awe of their dedication to the film, television series, or book. The same can be said for enthusiastic fans of entertainers, sports personalities, and games. Their loyalty is truly astonishing to witness. Speak poorly about their hero, and they'll discard you faster than a rotten piece of fruit.

Many will even idolize these "heroes." They dress like them, behave like them, speak like them, and take their opinions on almost anything as fact. They worship those false idols at the altar of delusion. And make no mistake about it; they will fight for the honor of the object of their devotion. Speak ill of them, or do even as little as wear the wrong color shirt at a sports stadium, and you may face a level of aggression that is hard to comprehend. For them, your inability to adore their hero or team only reflects your ignorance, and they will do anything to disparage you for your total lack of intelligence. Their dedication is so immense that they even identify themselves with names associated with their favorite hero or team.

Have you ever heard someone referred to as a "Trekkie," "Belieber," "Cowboy," or "Patriot"? In the Harry Potter series of movies, there were four wizardry "houses," and I know people who have taken tests to see which of those they belong to. They then proudly consider themselves a "Slytherin,"

"Gryffindor," "Hufflepuff," or "Ravenclaw." Now, a disclaimer. I'm not trying to shame anyone for enjoying a particular entertainment genre or following the adventures of a fictional hero. Kudos to you if that describes you. Enjoy it and have fun, but please don't lose sight of the forest of eternity for the tree of some fanciful character or team.

Most people can't name all the books of the Bible or the disciples, and even fewer can quote more than a couple of scriptures. Ask them about their favorite pastime, and they will impress you with their knowledge of it; however, ask them about the Bible, and all you get in return is a blank stare. Many watch the same movie or read the same book repeatedly, absorbing even the most minor details as they commit it to memory. Yet, those same individuals spend almost no time reading the Bible in a week. Few have read the entire Bible, and even fewer memorize scripture. They can be engrossed for hours watching games but cannot devote five minutes to studying God's Word.

Harry Potter, the Cowboys, or Taylor Swift can entertain you, but they offer little beyond that. They may help you through difficult patches in your life, but even that assistance is limited. They are mortal; as such, they are "here today and gone tomorrow." The hero of the New Testament is not bound by time; He is eternal. Harry Potter cannot provide you with everlasting salvation; Jesus can. The Rams cannot save you; Jesus can. Billie Eilish is not a god; Jesus is. None of them died for you; Jesus did. Be a fan, love the movie, and cheer for your favorite athlete or team, but remember who your God is.

Chapter 5
Faithful Thomas

"Now Thomas, one of the twelve, called the Twin, was not with them when Jesus came. So the other disciples told him, "We have seen the Lord." But he said to them, "Unless I see in his hands the mark of the nails, and place my finger into the mark of the nails, and place my hand into his side, I will never believe" (**Joh. 20:24-25**).

Today, I might step on the toes of many people who have read these verses or heard numerous sermons about the man who doubted our Lord and Savior. Most of us have heard someone being referred to as a "Doubting Thomas" for something they did not believe. However, before we are quick to label someone, we should understand more about them.

Was Thomas truly deserving of that title? We know he was one of the twelve disciples: Simon Peter, Andrew, James (the son of Zebedee), John, Philip, Bartholomew, Thomas, Matthew, James (the son of Alphaeus), Thaddaeus, Simon the Zealot, and Judas Iscariot. This means he personally witnessed much of what Jesus had done. He spent years following Christ wherever He went and learned countless lessons from His Savior. He was a personal witness to innumerable miracles, so why would he doubt the resurrection? It seems strange to us that, after seeing the dead raised, evil spirits expelled, the lame walking, the blind gaining sight, and water turned into wine, he would doubt his friend's claims.

However, this was not the only time Thomas had questioned something. Let's take a look at a scripture that witnesses that fact. **Joh. 14:2-6,**

"In my Father's house are many rooms. If it were not so, would I have told you that I go to prepare a place for you? And if I go and prepare a place for you, I will come again and will take you to myself, that where I am you may be also. And you know the way to where I am going." Thomas said to him, "Lord, we do not know where you are going. How can we know the way?" Jesus said to him, "I am the way, and the truth, and the life. No one comes to the Father except through me."

After reading this verse, we may wonder whether he was a doubter or someone who was more independent in his thoughts and needed clarification.

There is one more set of verses I want us to examine. When Jesus and His disciples received the message that Lazarus from the city of Bethany had died, they were concerned. They were not welcome there, and the disciples were reluctant to go, even reminding the Master that the locals wanted to stone Him. After Jesus informed them of Lazarus's death, "doubting Thomas" made the following remark in **Joh. 11:16**, "Let us also go, that we may die with him." Had it not been for the verses in **Joh. 20:24-25**, he might have earned the honorable title "Faithful Thomas." However, was he doubtful or skeptical?

Perhaps he was one of those individuals who needed to see something with his own eyes before believing it. As for that fateful day, remember, he was not with the other disciples when Jesus appeared to them. He was not just going to take their word for it: **Joh. 20:26-27**,

> "Eight days later, his disciples were inside again, and Thomas was with them. Although the doors were locked, Jesus came and stood among them and said, "Peace be with you." Then he said to Thomas, "Put your finger here, and see my hands; and put out your hand, and place it in my side. Do not disbelieve, but believe."

And for the record, Jesus did not call him a doubter. It could be argued that He was simply putting the disciple who always needed proof at ease. We all know people like Thomas. They are not necessarily doubters but are skeptical of anything they hear until they see the evidence themselves. What would our reaction have been had we been there instead of Thomas? Would we have believed the other disciples? Thomas had seen Jesus do all those miracles, but remember, it was that same Jesus he had seen crucified and buried. How would the one who raised the dead now raise Himself?

Moreover, why do we not call Peter a doubter when he tried to walk on water and failed or when He denied Christ three times? What of the disciples in **Mat. 28:16-17**, "Now the eleven disciples went to Galilee, to the mountain to which Jesus had directed them. And when they saw him they worshiped him, but some doubted." So, is the label "doubting Thomas" fair or not?

Chapter 6
Walking on Water

"And in the fourth watch of the night he came to them, walking on the sea. But when the disciples saw him walking on the sea, they were terrified, and said, "It is a ghost!" and they cried out in fear. But immediately Jesus spoke to them, saying, "Take heart; it is I. Do not be afraid." And Peter answered him, "Lord, if it is you, command me to come to you on the water." He said, "Come." So Peter got out of the boat and walked on the water and came to Jesus. But when he saw the wind, he was afraid, and beginning to sink, he cried out, "Lord, save me." Jesus immediately reached out his hand and took hold of him, saying to him, "O you of little faith, why did you doubt?" (**Mat. 14:25-31**).

We all know the story of Peter unsuccessfully walking on water. He started out determined, but no sooner was he outside the boat than his confidence left him, and he began to sink. We do that too, my friends. Granted, we do not actually step out of a boat and walk on water, but the concept of the story still applies. We live our lives in Him. We read the Bible, pray, and attend worship services, so we are faithful by all accounts. We love God and Jesus Christ, and He is the example we strive to imitate.

The Apostle Paul tells us to do precisely that in **1Co. 11:1**, "Be imitators of me, as I am of Christ." Paul isn't saying, "Be like me," but rather, "Be like Him." We know we fail miserably because of our weak, mortal, fallen state, but that does not stop us from trying. People around us may even admire our Christian loyalty and speak highly of us in that regard. Life is good, and despite the setbacks, we are unwavering in our commitment to Christ. Then, one day (to use the analogy of the storm), with the wind howling around us and waves battering our boat, we see Jesus coming toward us, walking on water.

We are in the midst of a storm of life, and we are afraid. We are so concerned about our situation that we call out to Him. It is then that He says,

"Come to me." Maybe it is when we are called to step out and do something we are a little afraid to try. It could be signing up for a new degree program, military service, mission work, a new job, or a different personal path in life. Whatever the reason, we must step out of the boat and our comfort zone and "go for it." Jesus says, "Come to me. Do not hesitate. Look at Me, and don't be afraid."

We recite **Php. 4:13**, as we confidently place one foot out of the boat, "I can do all things through him who strengthens me." Life is great, and we are excited about what lies ahead. But no sooner does the other foot join the one on the water than an unexpected wind arises. A fierce wind, maybe even a storm, and just like that, we take our eyes off Jesus. And when we do that, fear sets in, and fear is the destroyer of faith. Our faith can no longer sustain us. It can no longer serve to keep us afloat, and we begin to sink. All the confidence is gone, and the beautiful future we were once set on suddenly disappears like a mirage in the desert.

Don't let that happen to you. Don't let the devil use a fierce wind to instill fear in you. Don't take your eyes off Jesus. Keep reciting, "I can do all things through Him who strengthens me," while putting one foot in front of the other. Jesus has not suddenly left you to a miserable, drowning fate. He is still there, arms outstretched, ready to embrace you whether you have doubted or not. And if you have, Jesus is ready to grab your hand and pull you safely up out of the water – but only if you reach for Him.

We too often let setbacks deter us from our goals. We too frequently allow ourselves to be distracted, letting a seed of doubt take root. What if Peter hadn't been distracted by the wind? What if we weren't distracted by our own winds? What could we achieve if we kept our eyes on Him?

Chapter 7
The "Mystery"

> "Now I rejoice in my sufferings for your sake, and in my flesh I am filling up what is lacking in Christ's afflictions for the sake of his body, that is, the church, of which I became a minister according to the stewardship from God that was given to me for you, to make the word of God fully known, the mystery hidden for ages and generations but now revealed to his saints" (**Col. 1:24-26**).

Have you ever wondered what Paul meant by "the mystery" that was hidden for ages before being revealed? This isn't the only occasion we're told the same thing, either. Some might argue that Paul was seemingly obsessed with this mystery, referring to it numerous times in his letters, including **Rom. 16:25**,

> "Now to him who is able to strengthen you according to my gospel and the preaching of Jesus Christ, according to the revelation of the mystery that was kept secret for long ages..." and **Eph. 3:1-5**,

> For this reason I, Paul, a prisoner of Christ Jesus on behalf of you Gentiles— assuming that you have heard of the stewardship of God's grace that was given to me for you, how the mystery was made known to me by revelation, as I have written briefly. When you read this, you can perceive my insight into the mystery of Christ, which was not made known to the sons of men in other generations as it has now been revealed to his holy apostles and prophets by the Spirit."

What the previous three examples all have in common is that they speak of a mystery that was previously hidden and then revealed, but it is not the only time Paul refers to it. In **1Co. 4:1**, we read, "This is how one should regard us, as servants of Christ and stewards of the mysteries of God." So, what is the "mystery" then? If we return to the opening verses and continue reading, the answer to that question is revealed. **Col. 1:27,**

> "To them God chose to make known how great among the Gentiles are the riches of the glory of this mystery, which is Christ in you, the hope of glory."

Even more illuminating are the words of **Eph. 3:6-9,**

> "This mystery is that the Gentiles are fellow heirs, members of the same body, and partakers of the promise in Christ Jesus through the gospel. Of this gospel I was made a minister according to the gift of God's grace, which was given me by the working of his power. To me, though I am the very least of all the saints, this grace was given, to preach to the Gentiles the unsearchable riches of Christ, and to bring to light for everyone what is the plan of the mystery hidden for ages in God, who created all things...."

What was not revealed in previous ages was that God would unite Jews and Gentiles into one body—the promise of salvation was offered to every person on earth. No longer were the Jews the exclusive "people of God." From that time, after the Jews rejected Christ, everyone on earth who sought God and was obedient to His Word would receive the gift of salvation. This was arguably Paul's mission after his baptism. **Rom. 11:11-15,**

> "So I ask, did they stumble in order that they might fall? By no means! Rather, through their trespass salvation has come to the Gentiles, so as to make Israel jealous. Now if their trespass means riches for the world, and if their failure means riches for the Gentiles, how much more will their full inclusion mean! Now I am speaking to you Gentiles. Inasmuch then as I am an apostle to the Gentiles, I magnify my ministry in order somehow to make my fellow Jews jealous, and thus save some of them. For if their rejection means the reconciliation of the world, what will their acceptance mean but life from the dead?

However, the "mystery" was actually revealed way before the New Testament. **Gen. 12:3**, "I will bless those who bless you, and him who dishonors you I will curse, and in you all the families of the earth shall be blessed." Finally, we can wrap up the mystery with the words of **Gal. 3:28-29**,

> "There is neither Jew nor Greek, there is neither slave nor free, there is no male and female, for you are all one in Christ Jesus. And if you are Christ's, then you are Abraham's offspring, heirs according to promise."

Thanks to Jesus, salvation became inclusive rather than exclusive. No longer was a single tiny nation the only recipient of His love, grace, and mercy; now, everyone has the hope of eternal life in heaven if they accept and follow God's Word.

Chapter 8
Mother's Day Should Be Every Day

"Greater love has no one than this that someone lay down his life for his friends" (**Joh. 15:13**). There was no greater love than that of Jesus when He gave His life for you and me, but there is also a depth of love that is hard to fathom when it comes to people. We all have special bonds with our mothers. They are the first person to love us, even long before they hold us for the first time. Lovingly, they stroke their extended belly as they proclaim their adoration for the tiny life growing in them. Studies have conclusively shown that fetuses respond positively to a mother's voice, calming them and even slowing their heart rate when they are restless.

I can only imagine how beautiful my mother's voice must have sounded as she sang to me in her womb. A mother does not have to see her child for the first time for an indescribable love to occur. That kind of love is automatic for her. And a mother does not fear death when it comes to her children. There are countless stories of brave women who gave their lives during pregnancy or afterward so that a child could live. I imagine one of the greatest fears of any mother is thinking that one day she will pass on from this life and there will be no one to love her children as much as she did. She also cannot fall out of love with them.

She cannot divorce or abandon them – there is just no part of her capable of doing that. Her loyalty is unmatched, her love unrelenting, and there is nothing she would not sacrifice for the safety of those she has carried, loved, and nurtured for nine months and beyond. There are also countless stories of women suffering significant abuse to stay and protect their children, waiting for the right moment to escape with them. The insults, the beatings, and the pain are willingly endured just so that it is not inflicted on her children. That is love beyond understanding –the measure of love given to every woman by God Himself.

Do amazing things, and your mother is your greatest cheerleader. Do bad things, and she will be disappointed and punish you, but she will never leave your side. Every day, as you are playing and she is working, cooking, or cleaning, you are on her mind. Tired as she is, she will never be too exhausted to play games, read, or pray with you. Night after night, you drift off to sleep to that familiar, soothing voice. And when you are safely sleeping, she will pray for you again. She will not eat until you have, will not buy herself anything until you have everything you need, and you will never see her complain about it.

She is where you run to when you are ill. She has the magic touch that can hug any fear away, and she has the same magic in her lips, kissing every "ouchie" until it is better. From the first time she touches her belly in loving anticipation, she has dreams for you that are way bigger than the ones you have for yourself. She will love whom you love, but if they hurt you, they better be aware of the fury of a "Mamma Bear." Mothers never appear tired, sick, down, or in pain because they hide it so that you don't have to worry. Her only concern is your happiness, and she will go to any length possible to ensure that.

Your first movement in her belly, the first word, first step, first day at school, and every other first in your life will be stored in her memory banks. As you grow up, she will recount those moments to you with a pride only a mother can have. She will be the closest thing to the love of God you will experience on this earth, and she will be the first love of your life - the Christian example of how you should love other people for the rest of your life. Every loss of a loved one hurts, but every person I know who has lost a mother says nothing hurts more.

The only more significant hurt is that of a mother who has lost a child – part of her heart will be missing until she is reunited in paradise with them. If your mother is still alive, call her on Sunday. If she has passed on, remember her lovingly, but also remember that she would not want you to dwell on the loss rather than the memories. Lastly, I know this is about Mother's Day, but if you are a mother who has lost a part of your heart, know that they are safe, happy, blessed, and patiently waiting for the moment when you will be reunited.

Love your mother; she deserves it for the way she suffered during childbirth and the tears she shed for you or because of you. Love her for how she cheered you on when no one else did, endured the challenges you presented her with, and especially her undying love for you during your teen years. That last one alone deserves the best you have in return. And try to show your love for her for more than one day a year – I'm pretty sure she would also appreciate it the other 364 days. Don't live to regret not showing her how much she meant to you because one day, she will not be there to hug you anymore. Don't wait for Sunday. Do it now because every day should be Mother's Day.

Chapter 9
Finish Your Spiritual Race

"For I am already being poured out as a drink offering, and the time of my departure has come. I have fought the good fight, I have finished the race, I have kept the faith... Henceforth there is laid up for me the crown of righteousness, which the Lord, the righteous judge, will award to me on that day, and not only to me but also to all who have loved His appearing. (**2Ti. 4:6**).

As Paul approached the end of his earthly life, he reflected on his spiritual accomplishments. He stated that he had "finished the race," much like an athlete.

Of course, if you have ever read the New Testament, you know that this was not the only time he used that figurative language example. **1Co. 9:24**,

"Do you not know that in a race all the runners run in a race, but only one receives the prize? So run that you may obtain it. Every athlete exercises self-control in all things. They do it to receive a perishable wreath, but we an imperishable. So I do not run aimlessly...."

Whereas the **2Ti. 4:6** verse refers to a race that has been completed, this verse speaks of a future race.

Paul impresses upon his audience that many people will participate in a race, but there will be only one winner. As Christians, we should view our spiritual service as a similar challenge. Paul is not implying that only one Christian will ever win the spiritual race, nor that we should compete fiercely against our brothers and sisters in Christ. Instead, he encourages us to see our Christian service as a personal race and to train with the discipline required to succeed. A long time ago, I competed in half-marathons. I trained three to four times a week and then raced on the weekends.

My determination to do my best drove me to train even in inclement weather or when I felt slightly "off." I knew I would receive a medal at the end of the race, and I trained with extreme discipline and dedication to earn that award. When the time came to compete, I was as ready as possible because I had remained committed to my training regimen. I sometimes traveled long distances to compete, but I knew I was not endowed with the natural athletic ability to win any of those races. However, that did not mean I did not compete against myself.

No matter how hard it became, I refused to let myself fail. Every race I finished in a faster time than before gave me such a sense of accomplishment that tears of joy streamed down my cheeks. That participation medal symbolized my success in conquering another week of watching my diet, training hard every day, and improving my abilities through discipline. But, beyond the joy of the accolades from friends and family, and even the medals, was the sense of achievement I felt after completing a race. It's not easy to describe the immense pride I felt as I crossed the finish line. I had stayed the course, done what I set out to do, and my prize was waiting. I can only imagine how great the sense of achievement will be when I complete my spiritual race here on earth.

Paul had endured hardships, suffered exhaustion, beaten the odds, and was about to cross the finish line. When he did, he would receive his prize—eternal bliss. That prize is immeasurably more valuable than any we can earn for finishing or even being victorious in our earthly athletic pursuits. Train with discipline, compete with determination, persevere with courage, and complete your spiritual race. Then, like Paul, you can look back with pride and forward with anticipation to the day you receive the "crown of righteousness."

Chapter 10
The False Promise on the Mountain

"Then Jesus was led up by the Spirit into the wilderness to be tempted by the devil. And after fasting forty days and forty nights, he was hungry. And the tempter came and said to him, 'If you are the Son of God, command these stones to become loaves of bread.' But he answered, 'It is written, Man shall not live by bread alone, but by every word that comes from the mouth of God.' Then the devil took him to the holy city and set him on the pinnacle of the temple and said to him, If you are the Son of God, throw yourself down, for it is written, He will command his angels concerning you, and On their hands they will bear you up, lest you strike your foot against a stone.'

Jesus said to him, 'Again it is written, You shall not put the Lord your God to the test.' Again, the devil took him to a very high mountain and showed him all the kingdoms of the world and their glory. And he said to him, 'All these I will give you, if you will fall down and worship me. Then Jesus said to him, 'Be gone, Satan! For it is written, You shall worship the Lord your God and him only shall you serve. Then the devil left him, and behold, angels came and were ministering to him" (**Mat. 4:1-11**).

Do not underestimate the devil. If he was willing to tempt Jesus Christ, how eager would he be to tempt you and me? He knows something we all should recognize: "Millions of people are more afraid of not being acknowledged by man than they are of God's judgment." That may seem strange initially, but look around and see how many people abandon the Gospel's teachings for worldly acclaim. Satan will take you to the figurative "high mountain" and promise you "all the kingdoms and their glory," but make no mistake; he has no intention of ever giving you anything.

This is not only because he does not have the authority to do so but also because lying is his nature. This is made abundantly clear in **Joh. 8:44**,

> "You are of your father the devil, and your will is to do your father's desires. He was a murderer from the beginning and does not stand in the truth because there is no truth in him. When he lies, he speaks out of his own character, for he is a liar and the father of all lies."

How can the prince of darkness, the author of evil and deceit, be trusted for one second? Christ did not fall into his trap, but so many people do that it can be disheartening at times.

The devil is cunning. He is a master of disguise, manipulation, deception, and evil, fully aware of your greatest weaknesses. Armed with that knowledge, he will lay a trap for you. Those empty promises of glitz and glamor, made so carelessly, will ensnare you. If you pay any mind to him, you will soon find yourself asking, "Why can't I have that new, shiny thing, that beautiful person who belongs to someone else, plenty of money, or a large mansion?" Give in to his hollow promises, and you will start to pursue worldly treasures like fame, fortune, and acclaim, accumulating fleeting wealth on earth rather than lasting treasures in heaven.

And he will offer you freedom, too. He will say, "Not only the kingdoms and their glory, but worship me, and I will give you freedom from the restrictions of Christianity. Worship me, and I will make you the god of your world." Sadly, millions fall for those lies, but they are not real. They think they will escape God and His rules and become self-proclaimed gods, but nothing could be further from the truth. Instead of experiencing freedom, they will be imprisoned; instead of gods, they will be slaves. The delusion will be presented to the thirsty traveler as a mirage in the desert. The promise looks real, but the reality is quite the opposite – you never reach the mirage because it keeps moving. In the end, you will die of thirst. It is as pointless as chasing a rainbow to get the pot of gold at its end.

This is the power of the devil – to exploit pride, envy, jealousy, and greed to draw people from the safety of Christianity into the darkness of sin and despair – leading to their eternal punishment. How tragic that the "here-and-now" holds more importance than the priceless treasures of the "then-and-ever after." How unfortunate that a brief time on earth is valued more than an eternity in heaven.

Chapter 11
Don't Join Them in the Dark

"Walk in wisdom toward outsiders, making the best use of the time. Let your speech always be gracious, seasoned with salt, so that you may know how you ought to answer each person" (**Col. 4:5**).

When Paul instructed his readers to "walk in wisdom toward outsiders," he was referring to their attitude toward unbelievers, among other things. In the previous chapter, we read the following,

"Put to death therefore what is earthly in you: sexual immorality, impurity, passion, evil desire, and covetousness, which is idolatry. On account of these, the wrath of God is coming. In these, you too once walked when you were living in them. But now you must put them all away: anger, wrath, malice, slander, and obscene talk from your mouth" (**Col. 3:8**).

Here, the reader—and by extension, us, are instructed to put away all ungodliness, for God's wrath will be directed toward those who continue such practices. Most Christians strive to adhere to all the commandments, which is admirable and certainly pleases God. As Paul himself did and urged us to do in **1Co. 11:1**, emulating Christ should be our primary daily goal. One reason we should strive to follow the Savior's example is presented in **2Co. 5:20**: "Therefore, we are ambassadors for Christ, God making his appeal through us."

The author tells us we are ambassadors, and with that title comes the responsibility of dutifully representing the kingdom of God. It is in our words and actions that God makes His appeal to seeking souls. Moreover, we are told the following in **Mat. 5:16**, "In the same way, let your light shine before others, so that they may see your good works and give glory to your Father who is in heaven." As ambassadors, our gracious speech, seasoned with salt and a godly life, serves as a light at the end of a dark tunnel for sinners. Lost, afraid, and confused, they stumble through the darkness of their sin.

With no moral compass, they do not know which direction to travel to escape the devil's clutches. Imagine their relief upon seeing the light and the promise of freedom from sin's bondage. However, ambassadorship is not the path all Christians take. Some profess righteousness, regularly attend church and other worship gatherings, yet behave like the world. Instead of shining as the light, they wander in darkness alongside the hapless sinner, indulging in the same vices that keep the unbeliever as a prisoner of the devil.

And don't even get me started on **Joh. 13:34**, "A new commandment I give to you, that you love one another: just as I have loved you, you also are to love one another." Some Christian hypocrites can recite this scripture but ignore it in their daily lives. They hate as easily as the world does and then claim to be better than the people they despise. Excuses like "They deserve it" or "I treat them the way they treat me" won't justify their actions on judgment day. They aren't ambassadors but an embarrassment to the Gospel with their shameful behavior. Furthermore, they cannot expect anyone witnessing their outrageously anti-Christian conduct to be drawn to the Good News.

We should remember that when we act like the world, we bring Christianity into disrepute. Often, the issue is our stubbornness or pride taking precedence over the Word of God. We lose sight of our Creator and replace His love and place in our hearts with Satan and hatred. Then, we effectively extinguish the light we are meant to be and ridicule our professed Christianity. Instead of being gracious and seasoned with salt, our speech becomes rude, crude, and abusive drivel, unworthy of being heard by anyone. Rather than our morally sound lives serving as a magnet for God's Kingdom, we become quite the opposite, repelling the seeking soul. Instead of seeing an ambassador, they perceive a worthless, so-called "Christian" who behaves just like or even worse than they do. As a result, they find no benefit in becoming a child of God. We will never attract people to Christianity if we do not emulate Christ. We will never win a soul for God if we do not show that soul a better way. Please don't leave them in the dark, but especially don't join them there.

Chapter 12
Will the Real Noah Please Stand

"Every word of God proves true; he is a shield to those who take refuge in him. Do not add to his words, lest he rebuke you and you be found a liar" (**Pro. 30:5-6**). As I read this verse, I remembered something that happened a few years ago. A friend told me about a movie called "Noah" that was available for rent. I didn't pay much attention to it because I knew such films were often factually inaccurate, but a few days later, he called to say it was a terrific movie. I was surprised because I had read online that it was simply horrific. Intrigued, I decided to watch it after all. Honestly, I wasn't expecting much, but to say I was appalled is an understatement.

It was a Hollywood adaptation of a Bible story, so I expected some creative liberty. However, nothing could have prepared me for what they did to one of the most beloved Old Testament stories. God had become upset with the people He had so lovingly created.

> **Gen. 6:12**, "...And God saw the earth, and behold, it was corrupt, for all flesh had corrupted their way on the earth." In the next verse, He tells Moses, "...I have determined to make an end of all flesh, for the earth is filled with violence through them. Behold, I will destroy them with the earth."

We all know the rest of the story, but there is one more verse I want to quote before continuing:

> **Gen. 7:13**, "On the very same day Noah and his sons, Shem and Ham and Japheth, and Noah's wife and the three wives of his sons with them entered the ark.

The story of the Ark is relatively simple and could be impactfully retold on the big screen using all the available technology in filmmaking. However, nothing could be further from the truth regarding this incredibly inaccurate version of the story. To say that the plot was lost in the making of the movie is a gross understatement. Not once does the movie mention the word "God." Instead, it uses the term "Creator." I assume that was intended to give the film a broader appeal and increase viewership, but that is not the end of it.

Noah wants to kill his family after entering the ark because he's convinced the Creator only wants the animals to survive. Staying true to modern trends, his wife assumes the leadership role and prevents him from destroying the last of the human race. Moreover, only one of his sons had a partner when they boarded the ark, and the king of that era was a stowaway. This absurd situation raises the phrase "based on a true story" to an unprecedented level of ridiculousness. The stowaway king also attempts to kill Noah near the movie's end. Oh, and let's not forget that the same king persuaded one of Noah's sons to help him kill his father.

Also, there are fallen angels known as "watchers," who are fantastical beings resembling walking rocks and are loosely inspired by imagery from the Book of Enoch. As if that weren't strange enough, after being persuaded by Noah's wife to intervene, Methuselah blesses one son's partner so she can conceive. Nothing mirrors the biblical story besides the name Noah, an ark, and animals. In the film, the animals are put to sleep with a magical smoke potion while a substantial furnace burns fiercely in a confined area on this wooden ark.

Here is the main problem with this story (aside from the inconsistencies). Similar to the series "Left Behind," many viewers will watch this movie and assume it is factual. As a result, they will end up with a completely incorrect understanding of a powerful narrative about humankind and our undeserved second chance. The harm these films inflict in the name of Hollywood's politically correct, profit-driven agenda is immeasurable. Although they may not care, a day of reckoning will come. Save your money and read the story from the only trustworthy source, the Word of God.

Chapter 13
The Attack Against Christianity

> "If the world hates you, know that it has hated me before it hated you. If you were of the world, the world would love you as its own; but because you are not of the world, but I chose you out of the world, therefore the world hates you. Remember the word that I said to you: 'A servant is not greater than his master.' If they persecuted me, they will also persecute you" (**Joh. 15:18-20**).

We often thank our soldiers, especially those who have sacrificed their lives, for the freedoms we enjoy, with religious freedom recognized as one of the most important. We are generally seen as a Christian country, and there is a widespread belief that everyone in America attends church. And why wouldn't they? Most towns have an abundance of churches, and we are frequently depicted this way in movies and television shows.

This is similar to all Americans believing that the entire Jewish population of Israel consists of practicing Jews. Unless you travel to a country and investigate specifically, you could easily be misled by popular belief. When it comes to America being entirely or predominantly a Christian nation, not everything is as it appears. Over many decades, Satan has systematically attacked the church in the halls of government and society, and he has even infiltrated our churches to attack them from within. Paul warned us about that in **Act. 20:29-30**,

> "I know that after my departure fierce wolves will come in among you, not sparing the flock; and from among your own selves will arise men speaking twisted things, to draw away the disciples after them."

Just as Jesus is "...the same yesterday and today and forever" (**Heb. 11:8**), so is the devil. Let's examine his persistent attack on Christianity in recent years, particularly in schools. In 1962, the landmark case Engel v. Vitale marked the first successful challenge against school prayer, ruling it unconstitutional. Then, in 1963, the notable case of Madalyn O'Hair (Murray v. Curlett) resulted in the complete removal of Bible reading from all schools. Interestingly, her son, William O'Hair, would later become a preacher and a strong advocate for reinstating prayer in schools.

In 1968, in the case of Epperson vs. Arkansas, the ban on teaching evolution in schools was deemed unconstitutional. In 1980, the Supreme Court ruled that displaying the Ten Commandments in a classroom violated the Constitution. In 1985, a moment of silence in schools was found unconstitutional if intended to promote prayer. In 1992, the Supreme Court decided that having a member of the clergy recite a prayer in elementary and secondary schools was unconstitutional.

In 2001, a federal district court ruled that a teacher could be removed from a class because they were creationists and could not adequately teach evolution. The intentional dilution or removal of anything Christian diminishes its significance. Over time, the loss is felt in society as more and more people become apathetic toward religion. Failing to introduce Jesus to the young may hinder their faith later on. We need to be aware that the church is under attack every day. Our freedom to preach biblical truth, share our faith with others, and pray in public, to name a few, may not be a privilege for much longer. We need to pray that evil does not prevail.

Chapter 14
Will You "Pay It Forward?"

> "For what can be known about God is plain to them, because God has shown it to them. For His invisible attributes, namely, His eternal power and divine nature, have been clearly perceived, ever since the creation of the world, in the things that have been made. So they are without excuse" (**Rom. 1:19-20**).

Before warning his readers about the dangers of approving the numerous sins listed at the end of the chapter, Paul reassures them of God's presence in everything around them. Many preachers and teachers have cited those words to argue that no one in the world has an excuse for not believing in God, but that assertion is not entirely accurate.

Before you judge me for misinterpreting the scriptures, let me clarify. For Christians reading those words, it's as clear as day that God is the supreme, omnipotent creator of everything in the universe—there's no debate there. However, if these two scriptures are taken from the Bible and thrown at an unbeliever, they may not understand whom you are referring to. Let's imagine for a moment that a person is sitting in a field somewhere in the world and starts to contemplate creation. They will indeed witness the work of a divine power, but they might not necessarily attribute it to the one true God.

Throughout history, humanity has sought to answer the perplexing questions of "the beginning of the world" and "the meaning of life." With a few exceptions, most people did not attribute all the glory around them to God but rather to numerous false gods. The Almighty, you see, does not sign His creations. You will not find His name branded on the skin of an animal like a rancher's mark on a cow. Humans do not have "Made by God" stickers on our skin, heart, liver, or kidneys, nor do the stars, planets, sun, moon, and earth. Thus, as humanity marveled at the splendor of the world and celestial bodies, it was only natural that they created gods to whom they could ascribe creation.

To satisfy his desire to know a higher power, man created that power and bowed down to it. Without the writings of the scriptures, who could blame him? We have an innate longing to know God, but without accurate information, we simply create one ourselves. It's sad, but it's true. Throughout history, thousands of false gods have been fashioned by those who have never encountered the scriptures. Unfortunately, none of those idols will benefit their creators. None can offer salvation. None possesses any power whatsoever. Now, let me ask you: how did you learn about God? Probably not merely by observing the magnificence of creation, but by hearing of Him.

Someone may have told you, or you may have picked up the Bible and read it yourself: it was the Word of God that provided you with the knowledge of your Creator. I mention this because we have a responsibility to ensure that those who have not yet had the opportunity will hear the words of God and have the chance to turn from their wicked ways. Salvation does not belong exclusively to you or me. Salvation is not meant for a select few. It was given freely to us, and we should share it freely with others.

Like your life, theirs will be transformed for the better, and they will receive the promise made by God to all those who believe in Him in **Act. 16:31**, "...Believe in the Lord Jesus, and you will be saved, you and your household." However, they will only have that opportunity when they either hear the gospel from someone else or read the Bible because it has been given to them. We can either speak to them directly, provide them with the Bible, or support missionaries who have dedicated their lives to spreading the Gospel in areas that are in desperate need of spiritual guidance. Do you want to save a life, or do you want to stand by and watch them suffer a spiritual death?

Chapter 15
The Temptations of Jesus

"And Jesus, full of the Holy Spirit, returned from the Jordan and was led by the Spirit in the wilderness for forty days, being tempted by the devil. And he ate nothing during those days. And when they were ended, he was hungry. The devil said to him, "If you are the Son of God, command this stone to become bread." And Jesus answered him, "It is written, 'Man shall not live by bread alone.'" And the devil took him up and showed him all the kingdoms of the world in a moment of time, and said to him, "To you I will give all this authority and their glory, for it has been delivered to me, and I give it to whom I will.

If you, then, will worship me, it will all be yours." And Jesus answered him, "It is written, "'You shall worship the Lord your God, and him only shall you serve.'" And he took him to Jerusalem and set him on the pinnacle of the temple and said to him, "If you are the Son of God, throw yourself down from here, for it is written, "'He will command his angels concerning you, to guard you,' and "'On their hands they will bear you up, lest you strike your foot against a stone.'" And Jesus answered him, "It is said, 'You shall not put the Lord your God to the test.'" And when the devil had ended every temptation, he departed from him until an opportune time" (**Luk. 4:1-13**).

This is one of the greatest stories in the Bible because it demonstrates how relatable Christ is to us. You may have heard it said that the most exceptional warrior leaders are those who lead from the front. Leaders like that embody the true essence of courage and bravery. You may have also heard it said that business leaders should only ask their employees to do what they are willing to do themselves. The idea is that they can only understand the worker's plight if they have walked in their shoes, so to speak. It is also true that we have immense respect for leaders who are willing to show such courage and conviction.

Furthermore, it has been proven both on the battlefield and in the boardroom that those under their leadership are significantly more motivated to follow them into battle, regardless of the dangers, due to their example. Jesus was willing to place Himself in the path of temptation so that the great 'I AM' could personally understand what we experience daily. It may not be food we crave but rather money, power, and fame; nonetheless, we still experience hunger. It may not be that we bow down to worship the devil directly, but when we submit to the gods of money, power, and fame, we might as well be worshipping him. And it may not be that we will throw ourselves down from a high place, but when we step off into the abyss of sin and darkness, we are indeed throwing ourselves down from the highest place.

Unfortunately, we often believe we can prevent ourselves from getting hurt because we are in control, but nothing could be further from the truth. Jesus experienced temptation to understand our suffering, but He also demonstrated a better way than yielding to it. His resilience and strength against the devil's cunning tactics show us that with faith in God, we, too, can resist him who desires our demise.

Jam. 4:7 states, "Submit yourselves therefore to God. Resist the devil, and he will flee from you." Jesus proved that He is a warrior king who does not expect us to face temptations He did not confront. He fought the same battles we face, but those He battled were even more intense, as He confronted the enemy directly. However, we are painfully aware that we are not perfect; unlike our Savior, we sometimes give in to temptation. Thankfully, our leader is not only perfect but also gracious and merciful, so this will not lead to our doom if we are willing to repent.

Jesus' experience showed Him just how difficult it is for us to resist temptation, so He has great patience with our weaknesses—and we thank God for that. Thus, we do not worship a Creator who doesn't understand us. We have a God who sent His only Son to be one of us so He could know the battles we face from our perspective. Now, that is love.

Chapter 16
Happy Marriage (pt. 1)

"Let marriage be held in honor among all, and let the marriage bed be undefiled, for God will judge the sexually immoral and adulterous" (**Heb. 13:4**). Here are a few excerpts from a blog I read years ago. I can't recall the author's name to give them credit, but many people share their views today, so I want to start by quoting them this morning. "In today's society, marriage occurs when two people (usually a man and a woman) fall in love and choose to spend the rest of their lives together in monogamy. But did you know that wasn't always the case?

In fact, the modern version of marriage emerged only a couple of hundred years ago. In the past, marriage rarely involved love (most marriages were arranged based on income and social status), and most societies allowed and expected plural marriages with either multiple wives or husbands. With today's rate of divorce between 40 and 50 percent, coupled with the prevalence of adultery in many marriages, perhaps it's time for the concept of marriage to continue to evolve... 41 percent[1] of spouses admit to infidelity, either physical or emotional.

This leads me to ask, 'Are we really supposed to be with just one person our whole life?' ... Hundreds of years ago, life expectancy was a fraction of today's. When two people in their 20s got married, it was quite possible that one of the two would be deceased within 10-15 years... Today, however, that same young couple could be together for 60 or more years! Is it realistic to think that two people could be emotionally, mentally, physically, and sexually compatible for that long? Maybe the tenets of a successful marriage should not be whether the couple stays monogamous for decades, but rather whether the couple openly communicates about what their unique marriage will look like, what will be deemed acceptable and what will not, and then honoring that joint decision...

I always tell my clients to create a vision plan of what they want their marriage to look like and what they'd both be okay with...This will enable

---

1. http://www.kinseyinstitute.org/publications/PDF/Infidelity%20in%20hetero%20couples.pdf

their relationship to grow within the confines of how they, as a unique couple, define marriage...Having that kind of openness to look at the relationship is key to happiness and reducing the shame of hiding your wants and needs from your life partner...If marriage is a sacred union, we owe it to our partner to be honest with them, however complicated it may be.

In my work as a Hollywood life coach and spiritual teacher, I see many clients who are divorcing and cite adultery as the main factor...And when I ask why the adultery occurred, the adulterous party usually explains they felt emotionally disconnected from their partner and felt trapped—that the communication was gone...Imagine how many divorces and heartbreaks we could avoid if our culture were okay with having this type of open communication—the kind of willingness to allow the marriage to evolve into something both parties can agree on, even if it's not society's customary image of marriage?"

For Christians, much about what was written in the blog is problematic, but the main issue is the author's view on who defines marriage. Marriage is not a man-made invention. Society did not, over time, determine the boundaries of what constitutes a successful marriage. In a more recent article by Veronica Lopez, a sex and relationship editor at Cosmopolitan, she quoted these statistics from their readership: "22% 'aren't sure' about monogamy," and "8,056,993: The estimated number of unmarried partnered couples living together." TBC.

Chapter 17
Happy Marriage (pt. 2)

> "He answered, 'Have you not read that he who created them from the beginning made them male and female, and said, 'Therefore a man shall leave his father and his mother and hold fast to his wife, and the two shall become one flesh'? So they are no longer two but one flesh. What therefore God has joined together, let not man separate.'" (**Mat. 19:4-6**).

In part two of "Happy Marriage," we will examine the information the CDC/NCHS printed on cohabitation, marriage, divorce, and remarriage in the United States. While the information is older, the statistics are not dissimilar today.

By age 30, three-quarters of women in the U.S. have been married, and about half have cohabited outside of marriage, according to a comprehensive new report on cohabitation, marriage, divorce, and remarriage released today by the Centers for Disease Control and Prevention (CDC). The report, prepared by CDC's National Center for Health Statistics, focuses on individual factors and community conditions associated with long-term marriages, divorces, and separations. Based on interviews with nearly 11,000 women 15-44 years of age, the study also examines conditions associated with cohabitation, including the impact that pre-marital cohabitation has on marriage and marital stability. "We've expanded our analysis beyond the basic 'bookends' of marriage and divorce to look more closely at how the issue of cohabitation impacts the life of a relationship," said Dr. Ed Sondik, Director of CDC's National Center for Health Statistics. "At the same time, we've also attempted to look beyond the influence of individual characteristics and are looking more at the characteristics of the community at large to get a comprehensive picture of what factors impact marriage and divorce rates in this country. Among the findings in the report, unmarried cohabitations are less stable overall than marriages. The probability of a first marriage ending in separation or divorce within five years is 20 percent, but the probability of a premarital cohabitation breaking up within five years is 49 percent.

After ten years, the probability of a first marriage ending is 33 percent, compared with 62 percent for cohabitations. The study suggests that both cohabitations and marriages tend to last longer under certain conditions, such as a woman's age at the time cohabitation or marriage began, whether she was raised throughout childhood in an intact 2-parent family, whether religion plays an important role in her life; and whether she had a higher family income or lived in a community with high median family income, low male unemployment, and low poverty. The report also shows that marriages that end do not always end in divorce; many end in separation and do not go through the divorce process.

Separated white women are much more likely (91 percent) to divorce after three years, compared with separated Hispanic women (77 percent) and separated black women (67 percent). Meanwhile, the probability of remarriage among divorced women was 54 percent in 5 years–58 percent for white women, 44 percent for Hispanic women, and 32 percent for black women. However, there was also a strong probability that 2nd marriages would end in separation or divorce (23 percent after five years and 39 percent after ten years). The likelihood that divorced women will remarry has been declining since the 1950s when women who divorced had a 65 percent chance of remarrying. Data for 1995 show that women who divorced in the 1980s only had a 50 percent chance of remarrying. TBC

Chapter 18
Happy Marriage (pt. 3)

"Therefore a man shall leave his father and his mother and hold fast to his wife, and they shall become one flesh." (**Gen. 2:24**). In one of the previous articles, I stated, "Marriage was not an invention of man. Society did not, over time, establish the boundaries of what constitutes a successful one." When discussing marriage and its potential for long-term happiness, it's essential to recognize that humans were not its inventors. We didn't create the rules, and we don't get to alter them. Society has shifted its views on marriage, claiming to understand more than the Creator, and some of these ideas have been established as law by authorities.

But that does not mean God is sitting in heaven saying, "Well done, My creation. I got a few things wrong, so I am fortunate you are there to correct those flaws." Not only is this insulting to God, but it is also dangerous to one's eternal destination. The problem is that we have removed God's perspective on marriage and replaced it with what the world thinks it should be. As with everything, once we do that, it results in the moral degradation and ruin of those institutions. God is the gold standard for behavior, and the Bible is His guide for us to follow in order to achieve happiness here on earth.

The decline of dating, marriage, and parenting started with the belief that we have a better system than God. This more inclusive, less critical, and less demanding approach suggests we should do whatever feels right for us. If there is a recipe for disaster, that is it. We are entirely incapable of keeping the "moral boat" afloat because we keep pouring the waters of selfish desire, sin, and delusion into it. God intended marriage to be a beautiful union between a man and a woman that lasts from the moment they make their vows until one passes from this life.

> **Mat. 19:4-6**, "He answered, "Have you not read that he who created them from the beginning made them male and female, and said, 'Therefore a man shall leave his father and his mother and hold fast to his wife, and the two shall become one flesh'?

So they are no longer two but one flesh. What therefore God has joined together, let not man separate."

It is intended to be an institution of love and devotion, honor and trust, and happiness grounded in the belief that God created it for love and companionship. Since I am a man, I will primarily approach this from that perspective. The man is the head of the marriage, and he should keep in mind the words of **Pro. 5:15-20,**

"Drink water from your own cistern, flowing water from your own well. Should your springs be scattered abroad, streams of water in the streets? Let them be for yourself alone, and not for strangers with you. Let your fountain be blessed, and rejoice in the wife of your youth, a lovely deer, a graceful doe. Let her breasts fill you at all times with delight; be intoxicated always in her love. Why should you be intoxicated, my son, with a forbidden woman and embrace the bosom of an adulteress?"

Having a godly marriage does not mean it will be free from difficulties, as the trials and temptations of life will challenge it. Those times are as sure as the sun rising. However, with a proper spiritual foundation, the union should grow stronger rather than weaker from these challenges. Many Christian marriages have also ended, so labeling a marriage as such does not ensure its success. Referring to it as spiritual or godly will not stop either partner from succumbing to the temptation of infidelity if given the opportunity. Too many individuals view infidelity or "new flesh" as a trophy to brag about. TBC

Chapter 19
Happy Marriage (pt. 4)

"Then the Lord God said, 'It is not good that the man should be alone; I will make him a helper fit for him'" (**Gen. 2:18**). We have already stated that God is the creator of marriage, not man, and the verse above testifies to that fact. There can be no doubt—at least not for any professing Christian—that God is behind the idea and that it was created for love and companionship. However, too many people fail to fully understand this. The world views marriage more as a convenience than as a commitment.

As long as everyone gets what they want from it, all is well. However, when one or both feel that the other is not meeting their desires, they neglect each other. So, what makes a good, happy marriage? Love, devotion, trust, faithfulness, companionship, perseverance, communication, and most importantly, God. If He is at the center of your life and marriage, things will go well—not perfectly, mind you, but well. In other words, a God-fearing marriage brings happiness and contentment. Nothing is more fulfilling than a beautiful marriage where love, laughter, adventure, pain, grief, and loss can be shared, leading to growth as a couple.

My wife and I have a wonderful relationship because we recognize and thank God for His role in it. We believe that His will was crucial in bringing us together and that our lives have improved significantly as a result. However, that doesn't mean everything has been smooth sailing: we have faced our fair share of challenges. There are certain actions we take that have contributed to our happiness as a loving married couple. Firstly, we do not allow our tempers to dictate any situation in our marriage. This doesn't mean we never disagree, but it does mean we never let our egos interfere with the facts.

We have been married for 25 years and have never spoken a harsh word to one another. We have never cursed, insulted, or demeaned each other or raised our hands in anger or frustration. We resolve our disagreements with words rather than actions, so we do not leave the house, sleep in separate rooms, throw things, or pout for days on end. Not once have we gone to bed in a bad mood. We make a concerted effort to address issues within a reasonable timeframe. Additionally, we refuse to let the bedroom become a battleground, so we withhold nothing out of spite.

We allow ourselves to laugh at each other and ourselves, never taking jokes personally. I can be childish, so I'm always dancing for her, pretending to be tough, or doing something else ridiculous to make her laugh, and she loves it. We laugh a lot – really, a lot. We work, walk, cycle, kayak, raise our children and grandchildren, and attend church together. We are rarely apart and wouldn't have it any other way. This doesn't mean we don't take time for ourselves or forsake our privacy, but we never see our shared time as a burden or a penalty.

We don't hide our phones or set passwords that the other person doesn't know. We view being asked where we are as a concern, not an accusation. Complimenting the opposite sex is not threatening to us because we understand the difference between "admiring" and "desiring." Our trust in one another is implicit, and the challenges of married life have strengthened rather than weakened our love and commitment. We hold a belief we wish every married couple would embrace – life is too short to squander years, months, weeks, or even days on senseless arguments.

We understand and do everything we do because we know our Creator God has a plan for our marriage. And one last thing: whoever passes from this earth first will not leave the other with any regrets— their memory will remain untarnished by the silliness of wasted time spent in anger.

Chapter 20
No "Made by God" Sticker

"The heavens declare the glory of God, and the sky above proclaims his handiwork" (**Psa. 19:1**). The words of David in the Psalm above cannot be more accurate. When you consider the magnitude of the universe and the complexity and beauty of our galaxy, it is impossible to deny the existence of God. Who else could have placed the sun, moon, and stars precisely in the right places in the heavens? Who else possesses the power to transform nothing into such a magnificent masterpiece? How can all this be attributed to chance? Surely, it cannot, as there is overwhelming evidence to the contrary.

It's not only in the Old Testament that we find scriptures illuminating the reality of the Creator. In the book of Romans, Paul has just finished stating that those who are unrighteous before God do not wish to know Him, so they suppress the truth. He then utters these words,

> "For his invisible attributes, namely, his eternal power and divine nature, have been clearly perceived, ever since the creation of the world, in the things that have been made. So they are without excuse" (**Rom. 1:20**).

Like in the Old Testament, these words assure the reader of God's existence. His power is everywhere, clearly visible to those who are not deliberately attempting to deny Him. However, there is a catch. The glory and design of everything good around us can only be credited to God by those who know Him. What I mean is that if someone has never heard of the God of the Bible, they might mistakenly attribute the beauty of creation to another deity. This is evident in the thousands of false gods worshiped throughout history.

This was true even during Jesus' time and before His arrival on earth, when God's influence in human history was much more direct. I think of events like the Exodus, where God's actions were clearly evident to both the Israelites and their enemies. For nations that had never heard of God, the sun, the stars, and numerous manmade statues became their gods as they tried to attribute all the beauty around them to a higher power. Today, billions of people have at least the opportunity to learn about God, but that still doesn't apply to everyone. Left to their own devices, people will create gods for themselves.

Clearly, those scriptures do not suggest that witnessing the universe's beauty will automatically lead the observer to know the one true God. It simply indicates that one will recognize a transcendent power overseeing all of creation, time, and space throughout the past, present, and future. There is a God who created everything from absolutely nothing—a God who meticulously arranged the distances between the sun, moon, and earth, as well as the atmosphere, wind, rain, ecosystems, and all living creatures, including humanity, morality, conscience, and love. No manmade idol could have achieved this, and it certainly didn't occur by 'accident.'

It must be and always has been a God with infinite power, existing eternally in the past and destined to exist forever. God's name isn't written in the stars or inscribed on the bottoms of rocks. We don't see His signature etched on animals' bodies or beneath every bird's wings. There isn't a "Made by God" sticker on the heart of humanity, which is why we can only rightfully attribute all things in the universe to God once we have encountered Him. In other words, we must learn of Him through word of mouth or by reading His Word. Only then will the false god be dispelled, and only then will credit be given to the one true God and Creator of all the heavens, the earth, and everything within it.

Chapter 21
To Believe or Disbelieve

"Now Jesus did many other signs in the presence of the disciples, which are not written in this book; but these are written so that you may believe that Jesus is the Christ, the Son of God and that by believing you may have life in his name." (**Joh. 20:30-31**).

God inspired more than 40 writers over a span of 1,500 years to document their experiences or those of people they knew. As a result, we have an accurate record of the creation and history of humankind. The Old Testament chronicles the beginning of the world and contains prophecies about the future. At the same time, the New Testament serves as a guide for the present and also includes prophecies about the future.

Together, these scriptures serve as firsthand accounts of the reality and glory of God and His Son. Once we hear the autobiography of the world, we face a significant decision that will affect us forever. At that moment, we arrive at a critical juncture—a point where we must choose to believe or disbelieve what we have heard. We will stand before two paths and must select the one we wish to follow. One will be labeled "easy" and the other "hard." The easy path will lure us because it seems to be the most accessible and least challenging, but its outcome will fall far short of expectations.

The challenging path may seem daunting, narrow, and full of obstacles, but its conclusion will be precisely what we are promised. After a land dispute between their herdsmen, Abram said to Lot, "...Let there be no strife between you and me, and between your herdsmen and my herdsmen, for we are kinsmen" (**Gen. 13:8**). Abram then gives Lot the choice of land for his herds to graze on, and he decides to choose the "easy" one.

> "And Lot lifted his eyes and saw that the Jordan Valley was well watered everywhere like the garden of the Lord, like the land of Egypt, in the direction of Zoar" (**Gen. 13:10**).

His decision to move and settle near the city of Sodom would prove unwise, as God would later destroy the cities of Sodom and Gomorrah. While it was not necessarily a sin, Lot's choice highlights the dangers of making hasty decisions solely based on appearances. In **Mat. 7:12-14**, we are urged to carefully consider all the facts before making a choice

> "Enter by the narrow gate. For the gate is wide, and the way is easy that leads to destruction, and those who enter by it are many. For the gate is narrow and the way is hard that leads to life, and those who find it are few."

What seems to be the least challenging path will lead to eternal destruction, whereas the more demanding route will result in a glorious eternity with God in heaven. Unfortunately, most people will readily choose the road marked "easy" because it fulfills their temporary desires for fame and fortune. The only way to justify that decision is to reject the witness of the Scriptures. That is an unfortunate choice they make: **Joh. 5:24**,

> "Truly, truly, I say to you, whoever hears my word and believes him who sent me has eternal life. He does not come into judgment, but has passed from death to life."

Don't be a Lot. Don't choose what seems easy and promises quick satisfaction. Don't deny what offers a life at the feet of the Father forever. Choose the path labeled "hard" and enjoy the rewards of staying steadfast despite the challenges you will face.

> "Blessed is the man who remains steadfast under trial, for when he has stood the test he will receive the crown of life, which God has promised to those who love him" (**Jam. 1:12**).

Chapter 22
Why Do We Sing in Church?

"Oh, sing to the Lord a new song; sing to the Lord, all the earth! Sing to the Lord, bless his name; tell of his salvation from day to day" (**Psa. 96:1-2**). Have you ever wondered why we sing in church? I once heard a story about singing praises to God. A little boy approached his mom and asked, "What happens when we die?" His Christian mother replied, "We will go to heaven, my son." He thought momentarily and inquired, "What will we do in heaven?" She smiled down at him and said, "We will sing praises to God forever." Suddenly, he looked worried. "Forever? Are we going to sing forever? Mommy, I don't want to sing forever; I don't like it that way." much."

It's an amusing story, but there's some truth in it as well. Not everyone enjoys singing. I know people who would appreciate an entire service of just singing, but I also know people who prefer less singing and more reading and studying. Almost always, the decision comes down to one simple factor: the ability to sing. Those who can sing love it, and those who cannot, well, not so much. So why do we sing in church? Firstly, because God wants us to, and it pleases Him. It's no coincidence that praising God is mentioned so many times in the Bible: **Psa. 47:1,6,7**,

> "Clap your hands, all peoples! Shout to God with loud songs of joy!...sing praises to God, sing praises! Sing praises to our King, sing praises! For God is the King of all the earth; sing praises with a psalm!"

Secondly, because God deserves our praises: **Psa. 7:17**, "I will give to the Lord the thanks due to his righteousness, and I will sing praise to the name of the Lord, the Most High." Why would we not want to praise the God of all creation who deemed us worthy of the life of His Son? Consider this: He sacrificed His perfect Son to save us. **Psa. 147:1** states, "Praise the Lord! For it is good to sing praises to our God; it is pleasant, and a song of praise is fitting." Are we not duty-bound to praise God, who desires it for all He has done for us? Now, before anyone says, "That is all in the Old Testament," let me quote **Rom. 15:4**,

> "For whatever was written in former days was written for our instruction, that through endurance and through the encouragement of the Scriptures we might have hope."

Of course, there are references to singing in the New Testament as well, starting with **Eph. 5:19**, which states, "addressing one another in psalms and hymns and spiritual songs, singing and making melody to the Lord with your heart...." One of the things Paul encourages his readers to do is instruct one another through singing. There is a great deal of wisdom to be gained from the words we sing that are lifted almost verbatim from the Psalms.

Even some contemporary songs have great lessons to be learned. Of course, that is only true if we actually think about the meaning of the words. Too often, songs are sung without considering their meaning, which is sad because we miss out on their lessons. A similar idea is conveyed in **Col. 3:16**,

> "Let the word of Christ dwell in you richly, teaching and admonishing one another in all wisdom, singing psalms and hymns and spiritual songs, with thankfulness in your hearts to God."

Singing not only encourages us but also creates a sense of community and fellowship as we all lift our voices to God.

James also tells us to sing when we are cheerful. **Jam. 5:13**, "Is anyone among you suffering? Let him pray. Is anyone cheerful? Let him sing praise." Another reason to sing is to use that time to praise God and focus your mind on the worship service. You don't need to be a world-class singer, but you should sing. The person next to you might think you sound like a screeching cat or can't carry a tune, but remember, you're not singing to impress them. You are praising a God who hears your words and loves every note. Sing like you mean it, and sing as if He is listening... because He is. Oh, and one last thought: "Why do we sing verses 1, 2, 4? Why do we leave out one or more verses?"

Chapter 23
Repentance Is Not Optional

"And Peter said to them, "Repent and be baptized every one of you in the name of Jesus Christ for the forgiveness of your sins, and you will receive the gift of the Holy Spirit. For the promise is for you and for your children and for all who are far off, everyone whom the Lord our God calls to himself" (**Act. 2:38-39**).

If you ask people what "repent" means, far too many respond, "to ask for forgiveness." They believe that saying, "I'm sorry," "Come into my heart, Jesus," or reciting a prayer is all that is required. They erroneously think that God will save them simply because they have spoken His name while still engaging in their deplorable, licentious lifestyles.

They continue to live in sin—cohabiting, drinking, using drugs, cursing, and employing crude language—believing, "No matter, I think I am saved. God is obligated to grant me the ticket to everlasting life." That is not Christianity, brothers and sisters; it is a delusion from the devil, given to those who are already doomed because they refuse to take responsibility for the necessary changes. That may sound harsh, but being aware of what the word means and then acting inappropriately is dangerous. Therefore, one cannot be too firm in emphasizing the importance of understanding repentance for what it truly is.

There are two basic meanings of repentance in the Bible. One comes from the Greek word "metamelomai," which means "to regret," while the other is derived from the word "metanoeo," meaning "change of heart." When asked for its meaning, most individuals in the church will say "to turn from," which, while not an exact definition, is not incorrect either. Recognizing that a change of heart and regret for our actions should lead us to turn away from sinful ways shows that the common interpretation of the word is valid. God does not want us to spend eternity in hell; instead, He deeply desires for us to be with Him in a place of such beauty that humanity cannot adequately describe it.

So great is that desire that He would give His fallen creation a way of returning to Him: **2Pe. 3:9**,

> "The Lord is not slow to fulfill his promise as some count slowness, but is patient toward you, not wishing that any should perish, but that all should reach repentance."

In fact, God's love is so profound that He sacrificed His perfect Son to secure the promise of heaven for His most cherished creation.

> "For God so loved the world, that he gave his only Son, that whoever believes in him should not perish but have eternal life. For God did not send his Son into the world to condemn the world, but in order that the world might be saved through him. (**Joh. 3:16-17**).

While students of the Bible understand that repentance is not the only necessary step, they appreciate its importance for their salvation. God desires our repentance, and His longing for us to be with Him is so great that He commands it. He does not force us to, but the Bible makes it clear that obtaining the promises of heaven's glory is essential.

> "The times of ignorance God overlooked, but now he commands all people everywhere to repent because He has fixed a day on which He will judge the world in righteousness by a man whom He has appointed; and of this, He has given assurance to all by raising Him from the dead" (**Act. 17:30-31**).

Although the Day of Judgment has been set, we have Jesus as our Savior and the Bible as our guide to lead us to a better eternity. Therefore, we are no longer ignorant and must do what is necessary to escape the judgment that leads to damnation. Just for the record, repentance is not solely for the unbeliever who has a change of heart but also for the believer in Christ who has sinned and strayed from the Word. We all need it to be righteous before God and for Him to fulfill His promise of an eternity in heaven for us. All I can say is, "Use it (repentance), or lose it (heaven)."

Chapter 24
Keep the Knots Securely Fastened

"Therefore, we must pay much closer attention to what we have heard, lest we drift away from it. For since the message declared by the angels proved to be reliable, and every transgression or disobedience received a just retribution, how shall we escape if we neglect such a great salvation?" (**Heb. 2:1-3**).

One of the greatest dangers facing many Christians is the possibility of drifting away from their faith. The Greek word for 'drift' refers to a gentle sliding away of a boat from its mooring rather than a sudden movement. Years of faithful obedience gradually diminish as the memory of their baptism becomes more distant.

Diligent Bible study and prayer are often unconsciously set aside for less important pursuits, putting one's salvation at risk. How is it possible that someone who is baptized and then lives what appears to be a great Christian life can forsake the teachings of the Gospel for the ways of the world? Simply put, the devil will lead them away from their faith one small step at a time. This is one of his most effective strategies. If he acted too early or suddenly, they would rebel and stand firm against him, recalling verses like **Jam. 4:7** and fighting the devil's onslaught with all their strength might: "Submit yourselves therefore to God. Resist the devil, and he will flee from you."

The devil must employ a more subtle method to execute his pernicious plan of separating individuals from God's loving presence. Believing that the author of all evil in the world is incapable of devising a brilliant plan of attack is extremely dangerous. Satan misleads them in small steps of which they are largely unaware. Temptation gradually unravels the knots that bind their souls to Christianity until, suddenly, they are set free. Tragically, they drift so slowly from their spiritual mooring that they fail to recognize the dangers they face ahead.

The further they drift away, the more challenging it becomes to see the mooring, and before long, they are so far gone that they no longer know which way leads home. For some, realizing the dangers they now face on the open, stormy seas of sin may come too late. Caught in the storm of egocentrism, anger, hatred, and addiction, they risk drowning in a spiritual death beyond imagination. They are not "up a creek without a paddle" but "in the middle of the ocean with almost no hope." Faith is the rope that tethers us to God's grace and mercy, and obedience to His Word is the knot that secures it—so how do we neglect that?

How do we fail to notice that the knot is coming undone, putting us in danger of drifting away? As mentioned above, faith is the rope that tethers us to God's grace and mercy, while obedience to His Word is the knot that secures it—so how can we overlook that? Disillusionment with the false promises of a Christian life free from trials and persecutions, or the equally misleading promises of fame and fortune, can drive people to untie those knots themselves. Some find the mooring too confining and seek to break free from its constraints, resulting in them not only drifting but also paddling furiously away from the safety of their spiritual mooring. However, not all is lost, as there is a way back, no matter how far they have drifted or paddled.

God uses the prayers of others as a beacon of salvation, shining like a lighthouse in the dark. It will guide the lost mariner back to the safety of the mooring of grace and mercy if they wish to return. Some will fight with determination to make their way back. It may take them a long time as they struggle against the wind and rough seas, but if they look closely, they will find the lifeboat of repentance nearby. All they need to do is climb aboard and paddle back to shore.

Chapter 25
By No Means the Least

"He said to them, 'But who do you say that I am?'" Simon Peter replied, 'You are the Christ, the Son of the living God'" (**Mat. 16:15-16**). There are three types of confessions in the New Testament. The first confession that Christ our Savior is the Son of God leads to the other two. Without this foundation, nothing else matters, as the fate of anyone who does not confess this is eternal damnation in the fiery pits of hell. Confessing Christ as the Savior of the world is essential to being Christian, and it is the only way—and let me emphasize, "THE ONLY WAY"—to the glory of an eternity in heaven.

Is it the only thing necessary for assurance of your salvation? Absolutely not, unless you disregard the rest of scripture, fail to study the Bible, or simply follow the ramblings of someone who insists that is all that is needed. They will emphasize **Rom. 10:9-10** while ignoring all other scriptures to persuade you that nothing else is required,

> "because, if you confess with your mouth that Jesus is Lord and believe in your heart that God raised him from the dead, you will be saved. For with the heart one believes and is justified, and with the mouth one confesses and is saved."

If I asked you to read the vehicle manual while learning to drive and told you to focus only on the paragraph that says, "Press the accelerator to move the vehicle," what would happen? If you did just that, the vehicle wouldn't move, and you would never reach your destination. Ignoring the instructions for starting the engine and putting it into gear, among other things, is absurd. Most people would read the other pages and understand that additional steps are needed to move a vehicle forward or backward. Why, then, take two verses from the New Testament and disregard others that discuss hearing, believing, repenting, baptism, and obedience?

Confessing in this manner is not optional. It cannot simply be dismissed just because you believe it is unnecessary. You either confess the truth, or you will never behold the glory of heaven. The Bible highlights Christ's role in our salvation through various scriptures. For instance, we are informed in **Act. 4:12**, "...there is salvation in no one else, for there is no other name under heaven given among men by which we must be saved." Regardless of what any individual or group may think, there is only one name to call upon for salvation. God sent His perfect Son to redeem us, not some mere mortal who lacks the power to appease the wrath of God.

Why so many religious groups dismiss the power of Jesus to save them is beyond the understanding of anyone who has read the Bible. **Joh. 14:6** reads, "Jesus said to him, "I am the way, and the truth, and the life. No one comes to the Father except through me." An 'Amen' could easily follow this emphatic statement to emphasize its importance. Failing to confess the name of Him, who is God in the flesh, will lead to eternal anguish, and John clearly identifies who they are in **1Jo. 2:22-23,**

> "Who is the liar but he who denies that Jesus is the Christ? This is the antichrist, he who denies the Father and the Son. No one who denies the Son has the Father. Whoever confesses the Son has the Father also."

You cannot call upon the grace and mercy of God without first acknowledging His Son, and the only way to do that is to confess His relationship with the Creator. Do you want to be called a Christian? Do you want to go to heaven? If so, obedience to scripture requires you to do several things, among which confessing Christ is by no means the least. TBC.

Chapter 26
Types of Confession in the NT

"Therefore, confess your sins to one another and pray for one another, that you may be healed. The prayer of a righteous person has great power as it is working" (**Jam. 5:16**). In the previous article, I discussed the importance of confessing our Savior, Jesus Christ, as the Son of God. I noted that there are three different types of confessions in the New Testament, and the first leads to the other two. Today, we will examine the second and third types, beginning with confessing our sins to one another.

One advantage we have as Christian brothers and sisters is the ability to rely on each other to overcome our sinful behavior. It is an honor when someone approaches us to confess their sins, as it allows us to demonstrate our love for them. The Bible has this to say in **Gal. 6:2**, "Bear one another's burdens, and so fulfill the law of Christ." When someone comes to you, bearing their soul in an attempt not only to obey the Word of God but also to ask for your prayers, you are helping them bear that burden.

One mark of true Christian friendship is the willingness to pray for one another. Prayer works—not in ways we may always understand, but always for the furtherance and glory of God's Kingdom. When we confess our sins to each other, we are, by extension, confessing them to God. In the Old Testament, King David confessed his sins to God in prayer. **Psa. 32:5**, "I acknowledged my sin to you, and I did not cover my iniquity; I said, "I will confess my transgressions to the Lord," and you forgave the iniquity of my sin...." He expressed confidence that God would hear and forgive him, even though this had to be done under the cumbersome law of sacrifices.

However, the death and resurrection of Jesus changed that. His work on the cross paved the way for us to speak directly to God, and we should fully utilize that opportunity privilege. John clearly states that in **1Jo. 1:9**, "If we confess our sins, he is faithful and just to forgive us our sins and to cleanse us from all unrighteousness." If you have faith in God and His omnipotence, you must believe that He will forgive what you confess to Him. Remember, confessing to another person does not mean asking them to forgive your transgression – that is something only God can do. You accept responsibility for your sin by verbalizing it and asking your faithful brothers and sisters to pray for the strength to overcome it.

Forgiveness lies with God, not clergy, celebrated leaders, friends, or anyone else. The other type of confession is equally important because it is Christ's confession of us. **Mat. 10:32-33**,

> "So everyone who acknowledges (confesses) Me before men, I also will acknowledge before my Father who is in heaven, but whoever denies Me before men, I also will deny before my Father who is in heaven."

Another scripture, **1Ti. 2:5** says, "For there is one God, and there is one mediator between God and men, the man Christ Jesus...." Essentially, this means that if we are willing to acknowledge Jesus as the Son of God and His role in our lives and salvation, He will similarly acknowledge us before God. Our commitment to Jesus leads to Him advocating for us in a way no one else can.

When I think of Him confessing me to the Father, I imagine standing before a judge, trying to plead my case but failing miserably. If only I had a witness to speak on my behalf. Then Jesus stands up and says, "I will vouch for him." He is willing to do that for His flock because He is the shepherd who is ready to lay down His life for His sheep. That demonstrates how great His love for us is. How awesome is it that our Savior speaks on our behalf to ensure we receive a room in the eternal mansion prepared for us? However, we must remember that confessing without commitment is in vain.

Jesus will not speak for those who are not obedient to God's Word. Confess to your friends and ask them to pray for you. Confess to God and ask Him to forgive you. If you do, your Savior will confess you to the Father, which is good, my friend.

Chapter 27
Rushing to Their Demise

"Now the chief priests and the whole council were seeking testimony against Jesus to put him to death, but they found none. For many bore false witness against him, but their testimony did not agree. And some stood up and bore false witness against him, saying, "We heard him say, 'I will destroy this temple that is made with hands, and in three days I will build another, not made with hands.'" (**Mar. 14:55-58**).

Have you ever been falsely accused of something? How did it feel? I bet you felt angry. Nothing is more infuriating than knowing the accusations against you are false.

Jesus was not only falsely accused, but His accusers genuinely wanted Him dead. They were so determined to see the Savior destroyed that they were willing to lie to justify their means. It may seem strange or even downright ridiculous to believers that despite all evidence to the contrary, He was still accused of being an imposter. They did not just want Him punished for his absurd claims; as mentioned, they sought the ultimate, most severe punishment for Him. Did those who bore false witness against Jesus not read **Pro. 6:16-19**,

"There are six things that the Lord hates, seven that are an abomination to him: haughty eyes, a lying tongue, and hands that shed innocent blood, a heart that devises wicked plans, feet that make haste to run to evil, a false witness who breathes out lies, and one who sows discord among brothers."

They were guilty of more than one of the things God hates, yet they persisted. Why would they do that? There were two main reasons. The first was that despite plenty of evidence to the contrary, they believed He was a fraud and not the Messiah. The second was that they liked the status quo. They relished the power they wielded and were unwilling to relinquish it.

This upstart would obstruct their goals, and they would have none of it. So, they lied and devised wicked plans to eliminate Him, but they did not account for the possibility that He truly was the Messiah. To say they failed miserably would be the understatement of all time, but when He died on that cross, they must have thought they had won. Remember the story of Jesus when you are falsely accused. Patience will bring the truth to light, and the accusers will become the accused at that moment.

I had a combat instructor who would tell us, "Make sure you have the right weapon for the job and ensure you have the correct ammunition. Be patient. Don't act too quickly – the right moment will present itself." Truth is the weapon, facts are the ammunition, and patience will reveal your innocence. Like those who attacked Jesus, lies are hurled at you because of a hidden agenda. Similarly, as in the case of Jesus, your accusers will meet their day of reckoning. They will have to face the consequences of their false testimony, lies, and deception. Jesus did not let their claims deter Him from His mission.

He knew what He was commissioned to do and did it, aware that they were plotting His demise. He already knew victory was His, so their pitiful attempts to rid the world of the great "I AM" were doomed to fail even before they ever hurled the first false accusation. Continue doing what you're doing. Pursue your goals and pay no attention to their feeble attempts to eliminate or control you. They are planning your downfall, but it will be their own demise that they inadvertently rush toward. Don't act hastily or vengefully because the opportunity to vindicate yourself will come.

Chapter 28
Spare Them a Thought and a Prayer

"Now I rejoice in my sufferings for your sake, and in my flesh I am filling up what is lacking in Christ's afflictions for the sake of his body, that is, the church, of which I became a minister according to the stewardship from God that was given to me for you, to make the word of God fully known, the mystery hidden for ages and generations but now revealed to His saints" (**Col. 1:24-26**).

Paul starts this section of the Colossian Epistle with a peculiar statement. He declares that he "rejoices in his sufferings" for the church's sake. It seems odd that anyone would view suffering as a reason for happiness, but this underscores Paul's dedication to his fellow brothers and sisters in Christ.

Paul was in prison at the time of writing Colossians, yet nothing would deter him from the mission given to him by Christ–to present the Good News to the Gentiles. This shows that Paul was willing to offer guidance and practice what he preached. In **Col 1:11-12,** he wrote,

> "being strengthened with all power, according to his glorious might, for all endurance and patience with joy; giving thanks to the Father, who has qualified you to share in the inheritance of the saints in light."

Far too many people are quick to offer advice but are unwilling to 'walk the walk' when it comes to enduring the same hardships.

Not many of us will have to endure imprisonment for the sake of the Gospel, but we should remember the brave souls who have suffered that and worse. Their dedication to the mission field is so profound that they are willing to do whatever it takes to reach those still lost in the darkness of sin. At the risk of being slandered, imprisoned, tortured, or even killed, they still face each day with optimism. Like Paul, they enthusiastically spread the message of the Savior God despite the real dangers they face. Most of us complain when we encounter someone who hates Christianity and slanders or tries to belittle us for our beliefs, but that is all we have to face.

While it may not make the experience enjoyable, we should remember those who are facing the threat of violence and rejection. In his 2nd letter to the Corinthians, Paul writes something that always reminds me of missionaries.

> "We put no obstacle in anyone's way, so that no fault may be found with our ministry, but as servants of God we commend ourselves in every way: by great endurance, in afflictions, hardships, calamities, beatings, imprisonments, riots, labors, sleepless nights, hunger; by purity, knowledge, patience, kindness, the Holy Spirit, genuine love; by truthful speech, and the power of God; with the weapons of righteousness for the right hand and for the left; through honor and dishonor, through slander and praise. We are treated as impostors, and yet are true; as unknown, and yet well known; as dying, and behold, we live; as punished, and yet not killed; as sorrowful, yet always rejoicing; as poor, yet making many rich; as having nothing, yet possessing everything. We have spoken freely to you, Corinthians; our heart is wide open" (**2Co. 6:3-11**).

Living in relative safety, it seems unimaginable for us to grasp that there are people in the world enduring unspeakable suffering for the same beliefs we cherish. It may not feel real because we haven't witnessed or experienced it ourselves, but the truth is that the vast majority of Christians worldwide live in fear for their faith. Currently, intolerance in America mainly manifests as vicious verbal attacks, yet we are beginning to see a shift toward more aggressive behavior from those who oppose Christianity. Although we haven't reached that point yet, and prayerfully never will, as you face unwarranted attacks, take a moment to think of those who find joy in their suffering for the cause of Christ.

When you are called hateful, fundamentalist, bigot, or some other derogatory term, spare a thought for those who would gladly endure that instead of merciless beatings and other severe hardships. Take a moment to think of them and then pray for their ongoing courage and safety. And, if safety eludes them, pray that they endure their suffering with bravery and confidence in the knowledge that Christ's resurrection ensured their ultimate fulfillment victory.

Chapter 29
Psalms 23 (pt. 1)

"The Lord is my shepherd; I shall not want. He makes me lie down in green pastures. He leads me beside still waters. He restores my soul. He leads me in paths of righteousness for his name's sake. Even though I walk through the valley of the shadow of death, I will fear no evil, for you are with me; your rod and your staff, they comfort me. You prepare a table before me in the presence of my enemies; you anoint my head with oil; my cup overflows. Surely goodness and mercy shall follow me all the days of my life, and I shall dwell in the house of the Lord forever" (**Psa. 23**).

I can confidently say that this is one of the most well-known passages in the Bible. In fact, many of us who have attended funerals have likely heard it recited or preached at least once. Its words are beautiful, touching, and poignant—they leave an indelible mark on anyone who hears them. The shepherd mentioned in the first sentence refers to God, and our calling to Him serves as a profound testament to our personal relationship with Him. Once we have read through all the words, we arrive at another inescapable conclusion–that we trust Him implicitly.

What most people overlook is the metaphor of the shepherd. However, in the Psalm, a deeper meaning is intended—one that goes beyond a simple peasant shepherd. It also serves as a royal metaphor. In the ancient Near East, kings were often portrayed as shepherds, as illustrated in **1Ki. 22:17** and **Eze. 34:1-10**. The ruler would provide for and protect the subjects in his kingdom and ensure justice for all, but he could not address the spiritual needs of the people. The only one who could do that was, and still is, "the King of the ages, immortal, invisible, the only God..." (**1Ti. 1:17**).

The theme of the shepherd King also continues in the NT, where Jesus is referred to as both. **Rev. 19:16**, "On his robe and thigh he has a name written, King of kings and Lord of lords." The words of **Rev. 19** clearly present Christ as the king of all kings, while **Joh. 10:11-16** speaks of Him as the shepherd of His flock,

> "I am the good shepherd. The good shepherd lays down his life for the sheep. He who is a hired hand and not a shepherd, who does not own the sheep, sees the wolf coming and leaves the sheep and flees, and the wolf snatches them and scatters them. He flees because he is a hired hand and cares nothing for the sheep. I am the good shepherd. I know my own and my own know me, just as the Father knows me and I know the Father; and I lay down my life for the sheep. And I have other sheep that are not of this fold. I must bring them also, and they will listen to my voice. So there will be one flock, one shepherd."

Since Jesus is God, the great I Am, He serves as our shepherd, just as God was the shepherd of the nation of Israel. In the past, actual shepherds were responsible for protecting the sheep. They were so dedicated to keeping the flock safe that they would sleep near the pen entrance to ward off predators. Moreover, if any sheep were injured, the shepherd would carry the hurt animal to safety and nurse it back to health. In the morning, the shepherd would guide the sheep to the best grazing spots and watch over them, always prepared to fight for their protection.

If one were lost, He would leave the flock to find the one, rejoicing when He found and returned the lost animal (**Mat. 18:12-14**). When we read, "The Lord is my Shepherd," we embrace the title of His "sheep" and heed the call of His voice. We know our Shepherd, Christ, gave His life for us and rejoices when a lost sheep is found saved.

Chapter 30
Psalm 23 (pt. 2)

"The Lord is my shepherd; I shall not want. He makes me lie down in green pastures. He leads me beside still waters. He restores my soul. He leads me in paths of righteousness for his name's sake. Even though I walk through the valley of the shadow of death, I will fear no evil, for You are with me; Your rod and Your staff, they comfort me. You prepare a table before me in the presence of my enemies; You anoint my head with oil; my cup overflows. Surely goodness and mercy shall follow me all the days of my life, and I shall dwell in the house of the Lord forever" (**Psa. 23**).

Last time, we discussed the word "shepherd," and today, we will continue our study of arguably the most famous of all the Psalms. When I was younger, the words "I shall not want" really confused me. I was not raised in the church, so I only heard the Psalm at funerals. In my mind, it read, "The Lord is my shepherd, but I do not want him to be." I was too embarrassed to ask anyone to clarify its meaning, so I pondered the apparent contradiction for many years. Thanks to my English teacher, I noticed the semicolon at some point. This grammatical punctuation denotes two separate thoughts that are closely related.

Suddenly, the light switched on for me, and I realized it was saying, "I will lack nothing because the Lord is my shepherd." In the previous article, we learned that the meaning of the word "shepherd" extends beyond the role of a literal shepherd of sheep. It traditionally referred to a king who would provide for his subjects. Regardless, the context suggests that we, like sheep, have our needs cared for by the shepherd. Of course, this does not mean that everything will go perfectly. It does not mean that God will provide absolutely everything our hearts desire. It does not imply a new mansion, new car, latest iPhone, fame and fortune, the person we long for, or any other "want." It does not guarantee that we will never be sick or encounter difficult times.

Nowhere in the Bible is a life full of desires and free of all challenges promised to us. In fact, we are promised quite the opposite. **Joh. 15:18-20**,

> "If the world hates you, know that it has hated Me before it hated you. If you were of the world, the world would love you as its own; but because you are not of the world, but I chose you out of the world, therefore the world hates you. Remember the word that I said to you: 'A servant is not greater than his master.' If they persecuted Me, they will also persecute you...."

It is spiritually disastrous to teach those who are seeking that everything will be rosy or everything we ask for will be granted. Using scriptures like **Mk. 11:24** to back up the misleading notion that God fulfills our every desire is deeply misleading. **1Jo. 5:14-15** clearly teaches there is a further consideration,

> "And this is the confidence that we have toward Him, that if we ask anything according to His will He hears us. And if we know that He hears us in whatever we ask, we know that we have the requests that we have asked of Him."

What it means, then, is that God will supply what we need: **Luk. 12:24**, "Consider the ravens: they neither sow nor reap, they have neither storehouse nor barn, and yet God feeds them. Of how much more value are you than the birds!"

We further read in **Rom. 8:32**, "He who did not spare His own Son but gave Him up for us all, how will He not also with Him graciously give us all things?" This naturally raises the question: "If Christians are provided for, why do some suffer from poverty, famine, and death? Clearly, there are political, geographic, and socio-economic factors to consider, but I do not believe that God is saying He will take care of all our needs without exception. The phrase we 'shall not want for' is more spiritual than physical.

We have God, we have Christ, we have the Holy Spirit. What we possess is the assurance of victory despite life's challenges hardships. We find comfort in knowing that we are assured victory in life's struggles with Christ in our corner.

Php. 4:11-13,

> "Not that I am speaking of being in need, for I have learned in whatever situation I am to be content. I know how to be brought low, and I know how to abound. In any and every circumstance, I have learned the secret of facing plenty and hunger, abundance and need. I can do all things through him who strengthens me."

"I shall not want" also conveys a sense of contentment despite circumstances. Let me conclude today with this: God sent His Son, the Great Shepherd, to save us. This fulfills the meaning of the words "I shall not want" for the modern-day reader.

Heb. 13:20-21,

> "Now may the God of peace who brought again from the dead our Lord Jesus, the great shepherd of the sheep, by the blood of the eternal covenant, equip you with everything good that you may do His will, working in us that which is pleasing in His sight, through Jesus Christ, to whom be glory forever and ever. Amen."

Chapter 31
Psalm 23 (pt. 3)

"The Lord is my shepherd; I shall not want. He makes me lie down in green pastures. He leads me beside still waters. He restores my soul. He leads me in paths of righteousness for his name's sake. Even though I walk through the valley of the shadow of death, I will fear no evil, for You are with me; Your rod and Your staff, they comfort me. You prepare a table before me in the presence of my enemies; You anoint my head with oil; my cup overflows. Surely goodness and mercy shall follow me all the days of my life, and I shall dwell in the house of the Lord forever" (**Psa. 23**).

So far, we have examined the word "shepherd" and the phrase "I shall not want." Today, we will continue with "He makes me lie down in green pastures." You may recall me mentioning that my younger self was confused by "shall not want," wondering why I would not desire Him if He were the shepherd. Well, the following sentence added even more confusion. Was God literally going to force me to lie down somewhere? What if I did not want to rest in that pasture? What if I just wanted to keep going on my way?

First, let me explain the meaning of "green pastures." If you know anything about the climate around Jerusalem, you'll be aware that there is little that resembles what we typically envision as "green" or "pasture." When we see those words, we picture a lush meadow filled with beautiful, thick grass and flowers, but that's not the reality in that region. With moisture from overnight condensation and the limited amount of rain Jerusalem receives each year, many springs were available. Around some of these springs, there would be areas of relatively lush foliage vegetation.

The shepherd would lead his sheep to those areas, allowing them to graze to their heart's content. The animals would travel as they ate, often not finding enough grazing in any one place. However, a focused and caring shepherd would guide the flock to better pastures to ensure they received proper nourishment. He would also create a safe enclosure for his sheep to rest when tired. God is our "shepherd," and if we listen to Him and follow His guidance, we, too, will find what we need to meet our needs. The casual reader may interpret those words as suggesting an abundance of opportunity, but that is not what is promised.

God will provide for our needs, though not always our wants, and will guide us to discover even better nourishment. Our shepherd does not force us to lie down but instead serves as our refuge from the chaos of life. He offers us an enclosure, a spiritual "safe space" to protect us from outside dangers. We find rest in His arms, and He never sleeps or takes vacations. He never gets sick or finds another job, leaving us at the mercy of the elements. We have no reason to fear anything because He is ever-present. **Heb. 13:5-6**, "...for he has said, "I will never leave you nor forsake you." So we can confidently say, "The Lord is my helper; I will not fear; what can man do to me?"

But, and this is a big "but." Without God, even our best-made plans can lead us away from green pastures. Too many "sheep' start their baptism morning with a strong determination to follow God but then stray from His Word, falling into calamity along the way. We must allow His will to be done and follow His lead. Not only will we find the greatest nourishment, but He will be there to catch us and prevent us from falling when we stumble. **Psa. 37:23-24**, "The steps of a man are established by the Lord when he delights in his way; though he fall, he shall not be cast headlong, for the Lord upholds his hand."

We must stop trusting in our limited ability and rely on God's omniscience to find us the best grazing. We must allow the scriptures to guide us: **Psa. 119:105**, "Your word is a lamp to my feet and a light to my path."

Chapter 32
Psalms 23 (pt. 4)

"The Lord is my shepherd; I shall not want. He makes me lie down in green pastures. He leads me beside still waters. He restores my soul. He leads me in paths of righteousness for his name's sake. Even though I walk through the valley of the shadow of death, I will fear no evil, for You are with me; Your rod and Your staff, they comfort me. You prepare a table before me in the presence of my enemies; You anoint my head with oil; my cup overflows. Surely goodness and mercy shall follow me all the days of my life, and I shall dwell in the house of the Lord forever" (**Psa. 23**).

Today, as we continue our study of Psalm 23, we will examine the phrase, "He leads me beside still waters." David, the author of the Psalm, has just stated that God, the shepherd of his life, will make him lie down in green pastures. What he implies is that God will guide him to the best opportunities in life, providing a "safe space" amidst life's chaos. He continues by expressing that in God, there is peace. "Still waters" certainly do not depict a raging torrent. This evokes the image of a slow-moving stream gently winding through a beautiful, lush meadow on a sunny afternoon. Most of us are familiar with apps that offer soothing sounds, and almost without exception, a babbling brook is one of the options.

My wife and I enjoy cycling along a bicycle path that stretches from one town to the next. It winds through some of the most stunning scenery imaginable. The path runs through a hillside so dense with trees that they create a green canopy resembling a "tree tunnel." It then runs alongside a lake with picturesque islands and a backdrop of untouched mountains. We cherish this experience, and it "never gets old," but the one spot we always stop at is a stream that the bike path follows for a brief distance. The sound of water gently flowing over rocks and pebbles is truly soothing to the soul. No matter how tired we are at that point, the beauty and serenity of the moment make every moment of the trip worthwhile.

Sometimes, we pause, lost in thought and awed by the beauty of God's creation, before continuing toward the goal of reaching the end of the trail, feeling refreshed and encouraged once more. Such is a life filled with the glorious presence of God through His Son, Jesus Christ. Not only does the Lord of our lives, the shepherd who guides our every step, lead us to the best opportunities, but He also provides a peaceful place of rest. Life can be daunting, even excruciatingly difficult at times.

One trial after another tries to pummel our spirits, but when we find the peace of God, nothing else seems to matter as much anymore. **Mat. 11:28-30,**

> "Come to me, all who labor and are heavy laden, and I will give you rest. Take my yoke upon you, and learn from me, for I am gentle and lowly in heart, and you will find rest for your souls. For my yoke is easy, and my burden is light."

When things become overwhelming, our shepherd offers the peace and tranquility that helps us concentrate without distractions. Slowly, our spirits are lifted, empowering us to persevere through the storm and reach the sunlight again.

But there is more to "still water" than just rest. Just as the refreshing water of a stream quenches our thirst and provides life-giving sustenance, so do the pure, life-giving waters of the spiritual stream. When Jesus asked the woman at the well for water, she questioned why He, a Jew, would ask a Samaritan for water. Jesus told her, "...If you knew the gift of God, and who it is that is saying to you, 'Give me a drink,' you would have asked him, and he would have given you living water" (**Joh. 4:10**).

When we find ourselves in the deserts of life, psychologically, emotionally, and spiritually beaten down, tired, and dejected, at our wit's end, He is there. If we ask, He will give us the living water that provides immediate relief and prepares us for an eternity where thirst never returns. If you haven't yet embraced the peace and sustenance of the "still waters," you should do so now – you won't be disappointed.

Chapter 33
Psalms 23 (pt. 5)

"The Lord is my shepherd; I shall not want. He makes me lie down in green pastures. He leads me beside still waters. He restores my soul. He leads me in paths of righteousness for his name's sake. Even though I walk through the valley of the shadow of death, I will fear no evil, for You are with me; Your rod and Your staff, they comfort me. You prepare a table before me in the presence of my enemies; You anoint my head with oil; my cup overflows. Surely goodness and mercy shall follow me all the days of my life, and I shall dwell in the house of the Lord forever" (**Psa. 23**).

Today, we will continue our study of Psalms 23 by examining the phrase, "He restores my soul." It may seem strange to a casual reader that we need restoration, even though, as His sheep, we dwell in His presence. However, the truth is that we all experience times of being downtrodden. Reflecting on the words for today's lesson, I recalled an unusual thing about sheep that I observed while growing up. We lived in a relatively small town surrounded by farms, and sometimes, my friends and I would ride our bicycles past the farms. At least once, we saw a sheep lying 'upside down,' unable to right itself up.

I remember the farmer or his helper being close enough to help the unfortunate animal recover. We didn't think much of it then, but later, I encountered the phenomenon again and decided to look it up. It turns out this is not an uncommon occurrence for sheep, especially when their fleece is at its thickest, making their backs quite wide. If a sheep becomes unbalanced and falls, it cannot generate enough momentum to roll back onto its feet. The condition is common enough that an animal in that predicament is said to be "cast."

What may seem funny to you and me can be life-threatening to it. Predators may take advantage of its plight, or the stress could overwhelm it. Without the shepherd's timely assistance, the frightened animal could perish. One of the responsibilities of a dedicated shepherd is to keep a close watch on the welfare of his flock to ensure they do not fall, or if they do, that he is close enough to rescue the terrified animal. In **1Co. 10:12**, Paul has a dire warning for Christians, "Therefore let anyone who thinks that he stands take heed lest he fall." Like the unfortunate sheep, we may become overwhelmed and stumble when temptations pile up.

However, unlike the sheep, our plight is not due to natural causes but the cunning schemes of the evil one. **1Pe. 5:8**, "Be sober-minded; be watchful. Your adversary the devil prowls around like a roaring lion, seeking someone to devour." When those times come, and they almost certainly will, He is there to help us back on our feet and "restore our soul." As mentioned in a previous article, our Shepherd never sleeps or takes vacations. He never gets sick or leaves us at the mercy of the elements (or temptations) for another job. We need not fear anything because He is ever-present.

Heb. 13:5-6, "...for he has said, "I will never leave you nor forsake you." So we can confidently say, "The Lord is my helper; I will not fear; what can man do to me?" Though we may stumble at times, we must remember that we are not powerless against the devil's attacks. We have the strength to free ourselves from the ever-growing "fleece" of temptations piling up on us. With God as our shepherd, we can escape the insidious onslaught. **1Co. 10:13**,

> "No temptation has overtaken you that is not common to man. God is faithful, and he will not let you be tempted beyond your ability, but with the temptation he will also provide the way of escape, that you may be able to endure it."

Study the Word, stay in it, remain obedient, and resist the devil. When you fall, look around. Through His Son, Christ Jesus, God is right beside you, arms outstretched, ready to lift you up—but only if you call on His name. If you find yourself on your back, overwhelmed by the weight of temptation and having lost your spiritual balance, call on His name in prayer. Do it now!

Chapter 34
Psalms 23 (pt. 6)

"The Lord is my shepherd; I shall not want. He makes me lie down in green pastures. He leads me beside still waters. He restores my soul. He leads me in paths of righteousness for his name's sake. Even though I walk through the valley of the shadow of death, I will fear no evil, for You are with me; Your rod and Your staff, they comfort me. You prepare a table before me in the presence of my enemies; You anoint my head with oil; my cup overflows. Surely goodness and mercy shall follow me all the days of my life, and I shall dwell in the house of the Lord forever" (**Psa. 23**).

Continuing our study of Psalm 23, today we will examine the phrase, "He leads me in the paths of righteousness for his name's sake." In the first part of the verse, the author emphasizes how we should walk if we are to be considered one of his sheep. In ancient times, a shepherd had to move his flock from one area to another, but that did not guarantee an easy path. Despite the challenges posed by dangers such as predators and rocky trails, following him would lead to safety and better grazing opportunities. Sheep that did not heed his voice and strayed from the path risked harm from the rough terrain or predators.

Today, many people choose to go their own way. They take the Bible, skim through its pages, and then, without careful thought, select the path they believe is best—the easiest one for them. The problem is that the easiest path is rarely the best. **Mat. 7:13-14**,

> "Enter by the narrow gate. For the gate is wide and the way is easy that leads to destruction, and those who enter by it are many. For the gate is narrow and the way is hard that leads to life, and those who find it are few."

Those who choose their own path, the one that is widest and looks easiest, unwittingly lead themselves to ruin.

The right way may seem small and the directions difficult, but following our Creator Shepherd will ultimately lead us to the best destination. Unfortunately, those entrusted with leading God's flock, such as ministers, elders, and teachers, often contribute to the problem. Instead of guiding the sheep in the way of the Lord, they choose a path of their own design—often intentionally. Those leaders should read and understand **Gal. 1:8-9** because the fate of the flock, and especially their own, is at stake:

> "But even if we or an angel from heaven should preach to you a gospel contrary to the one we preached to you, let him be accursed. As we have said before, so now I say again: If anyone is preaching to you a gospel contrary to the one you received, let him be accursed."

They should also read "**Jam. 3:1**, "Not many of you should become teachers, my brothers, for you know that we who teach will be judged with greater strictness." The second part of the verse reads, "For his name's sake." The shepherd did not exist for the sheep's benefit; rather, the sheep existed for his. They were expected to yield a profit for him. We live for God's glory, not our own. Like the shepherds of old, God provides safety and security, leading us to the best grazing for His benefit, which benefits us.

The sheep that stray do so for their profit, which alters the fundamental relationship with God from one of dependence to one of idolatry. Our actions reflect His kingdom, and we are called to obedience so that His name is glorified. We need to stop making Christianity about us – it isn't. **Mat. 5:14-16,**

> "You are the light of the world. A city set on a hill cannot be hidden. Nor do people light a lamp and put it under a basket, but on a stand, and it gives light to all in the house. In the same way, let your light shine before others, so that they may see your good works and give glory to your Father who is in heaven."

As we travel along the paths of righteousness, our light shines for others, guiding them as a lighthouse guides a ship storm. When they see our light, they find a way to escape the perils of the darkness of sin surrounding them. By following the path of righteousness, you will tread the steps of good people who have walked this way before you. Additionally, you will provide others an opportunity to reach the best destination as you illuminate their journey well. **Pro. 2:20**, "So you will walk in the way of the good and keep to the paths of the righteous." Be that light today by following the "paths of righteousness for His name's sake."

Chapter 35
Psalms 23 (pt. 7)

"The Lord is my shepherd; I shall not want. He makes me lie down in green pastures. He leads me beside still waters. He restores my soul. He leads me in paths of righteousness for his name's sake. Even though I walk through the valley of the shadow of death, I will fear no evil, for You are with me; Your rod and Your staff, they comfort me. You prepare a table before me in the presence of my enemies; You anoint my head with oil; my cup overflows. Surely goodness and mercy shall follow me all the days of my life, and I shall dwell in the house of the Lord forever" (**Psa. 23**).

In our ongoing study of Psalms 23, we will examine, "Even though I walk through the valley of the shadow of death, I will fear no evil, for You are with me; Your rod and Your staff, they comfort me...." Without a doubt, this is one of the most famous of all the verses in the Bible. This is one of the verses often associated with funerals worldwide, and I am sure we have all heard it preached at one time or another. But what does it mean? Sheep have no concept of death. They do not understand that their actions, which go against the shepherd's directions, will lead to their demise. They are blissfully unaware of the dangers of a wandering mindset – of trying to do things their way.

But the shepherd is not. He carries a large stick to protect them from danger, especially as day turns to night and darkness hides the evil that lurks within it. The author originally used the Hebrew word "salmawet," meaning "deep darkness." When it was translated, it was clarified with two words: "sel," meaning "shadow," and "mawet," meaning "death." They would finish it by saying, "Valley of the shadow of death." As we now understand, the author describes death—our mortality and our comprehension of it. Apart from those who are alive when Jesus makes His triumphant return, we will all die.

That is as fundamental a fact of life as breathing. No amount of money, education, wisdom, good looks, luck, or bargaining can help us escape it, and for most people on Earth, this is a frightening reality. Dying is said to be humanity's greatest fear, but it doesn't have to be, the writer asserts. He is confident that when death approaches; when he walks through the deep darkness, the valley of the shadow of death—his Shepherd will be with him. This fear of dying often stems from a fear of the unknown. What really happens to us when we die? David says, "Since you have God, you know what will happen, so why fear?"

Your Shepherd is with you every step of the way. Not only at the time of our death, but also before that, as we travel the final miles to that moment, He is by our side. Like a good shepherd, His rod and staff offer us comfort, assuring us of His protection. Instead of fearing death, we should fear not truly living. Instead of fearing the evil that can harm or hasten our demise, we should embrace the reality of God's presence and enjoy life. That understanding eliminates fear and anxiety, replacing them with a comfort only He can provide. Sheep do not comprehend death, which is why they don't realize they should live every moment as if it could be their last. But we who are aware of it have the opportunity to live our best lives and make every second count.

Moreover, knowing that God is with us also means He was with our loved ones before they passed away. Not only is it comforting to know we are going to be okay, but it is also reassuring to know they are, too. I am sure my dad doesn't remember this anymore. I don't think I've ever told him, but maybe he will read this and recall. I was young, perhaps 4 or 5 years old. My dad took me to visit a friend who worked in a tire factory. To this day, I vividly recall that factory's horrendous smell and booming sounds. The sounds, the smells, and the unfamiliarity of that dirty, intimidating factory overwhelmed me. I remember my dad picking me up, and I buried my head in his neck. I could feel his arms around me and smell his cologne, which calmed me – I felt safe. To this day, I love the scent of Old Spice.

How much safer am I in the arms of the omnipotent Creator God? I fear no evil, and I know that when my time comes to walk through the valley of the shadow of death, He will lift me up, and I will feel His arms around me... and I will know I am safe.

Chapter 36
Psalms 23 (pt. 8)

"The Lord is my shepherd; I shall not want. He makes me lie down in green pastures. He leads me beside still waters. He restores my soul. He leads me in paths of righteousness for his name's sake. Even though I walk through the valley of the shadow of death, I will fear no evil, for You are with me; Your rod and Your staff, they comfort me. You prepare a table before me in the presence of my enemies; You anoint my head with oil; my cup overflows. Surely goodness and mercy shall follow me all the days of my life, and I shall dwell in the house of the Lord forever" (**Psa. 23**).

Today, as we continue our study of Psalm 23, we will examine the verse, "You prepare a table before me in the presence of my enemies; You anoint my head with oil; my cup overflows...." Many believe that "You prepare a table before me" serves as an analogy for a shepherd feeding his flock. In this metaphor, the table represents a trough filled with feed, generously spread out. The "enemies" signify predators who must watch helplessly as the all-powerful shepherd they fear protects his sheep. The anointing of the head with oil indicates the treatment of wounds, and the phrase "my cup overflows" reflects the abundance of water available for the thirsty sheep.

While I have no issue with the aforementioned, I prefer to view it as a transition from the shepherd analogy to that of an actual banquet. The phrase "prepare a table before me" is also found in the Old Testament. In **Psa. 78:18-19**, the author refers to Israel questioning whether God could provide for them after the "Great Escape" from Egypt – "They tested God in their heart by demanding the food they craved. They spoke against God, saying, "Can God spread a table in the wilderness?" They wanted to know if God could provide for their daily nutritional needs.

In Psalms 23, the table is not only prepared but also done so in the presence of His enemies. The inclusion of "in the presence of my enemies" means the Lord provides not only nutrition but also everything David needs to be victorious over them. He was never alone: **Heb. 13:6**, "So we can confidently say, "The Lord is my helper; I will not fear; what can man [or evil] do to me?"

As I studied the meaning of "anoint," I realized there are many interpretations. One scholar believes it signifies the indwelling of the Holy Spirit within us. Another thinks it represents God's blessings, while yet another believes it refers to the tools needed to conquer our enemies. Let us return briefly to the sheep analogy. The animals could be tormented by flies that lay eggs in their nostrils, and their eyes and ears could also be targeted by pesky insects. To prevent this, the shepherd would pour oil over the head of the sheep to serve as a barrier against these attacks.

When David spoke of the anointing, he may well have meant that God provides us with the tools to resist or overcome the attacks of our enemies. **2Co. 1:20-21**,

> "For all the promises of God find their Yes in him. That is why it is through him that we utter our Amen to God for his glory. And it is God who establishes us with you in Christ, and has anointed us...."

Lastly, "my cup overflows" refers to the abundance of our portion. While studying this Psalm, I discovered an interesting fact that supports this idea. In ancient hospitality, hosts would deliberately overfill guests' cups as a gesture, inviting them to stay as long as they wished. This is a beautiful thought when we consider Psalm 23. God provides for our every need in abundance and wants us to know we are welcome to stay as long as we like. When we are baptized into Christ, we have more than we will ever need and can never overstay our welcome. I want to conclude with two scriptures that perfectly illustrate everything I have said today: **Mat. 6:26, 30**,

> "Look at the birds of the air: they neither sow nor reap nor gather into barns, and yet your heavenly Father feeds them. Are you not of more value than they?... But if God so clothes the grass of the

field, which today is alive and tomorrow is thrown into the oven, will he not much more clothe you...."

Heb. 13:5b, "He will never leave us, "...for he has said, "I will never leave you nor forsake you."

Chapter 37
Psalms 23 (pt. 9)

"The Lord is my shepherd; I shall not want. He makes me lie down in green pastures. He leads me beside still waters. He restores my soul. He leads me in paths of righteousness for his name's sake. Even though I walk through the valley of the shadow of death, I will fear no evil, for You are with me; Your rod and Your staff, they comfort me. You prepare a table before me in the presence of my enemies; You anoint my head with oil; my cup overflows. Surely goodness and mercy shall follow me all the days of my life, and I shall dwell in the house of the Lord forever" (**Psa. 23**).

In our last installment on the meaning of Psalm 23, we will examine, "Surely goodness and mercy shall follow me all the days of my life, and I shall dwell in the house of the Lord forever." The psalmist now summarizes the benefits of being a sheep in the Lord's flock and an honored guest at a table set for them. When we are in Christ—the only way to the Father—we walk in righteousness, and God's blessings (goodness and mercy) follow us 'all the days of our lives.' This does not imply that our journey will be without challenges, but it assures us that He will be with us every step of the way.

He knows where the best grazing is and will lead us there while protecting us from the predatory attacks of the evil one. But, even when we stray, He will be merciful and receive us back into the flock, forgiving our wandering spirit. We are assured that trials will come our way. **Joh. 15:20**, "Remember the word that I said to you: 'A servant is not greater than his master.' If they persecuted me, they will also persecute you." Now, that may sound harsh, but when viewed through the correct lens, one sees those persecutions from a different perspective – a perspective that shows purpose. **1Pe. 1:6-7**,

> "In this you rejoice, though now for a little while, if necessary, you have been grieved by various trials, so that the tested genuineness

of your faith—more precious than gold that perishes though it is tested by fire—may be found to result in praise and glory and honor at the revelation of Jesus Christ."

When we face tests, our faith is often tested, resulting in us being either Fairweather Christians or devoted followers, faithful children of the Most High God. Additionally, challenges have another purpose, as explained in **Jam. 1:2-4**,

"Count it all joy, my brothers, when you meet trials of various kinds, for you know that the testing of your faith produces steadfastness. And let steadfastness have its full effect, that you may be perfect and complete, lacking in nothing."

The path to heaven is strewn with trials. Some trials are small, some are large, and others seem monumental. However, overcoming them strengthens us, deepens our faith, and inspires others through our perseverance. No matter the challenge, God's blessings—whether small, large, or monumental—are bestowed upon us in proportion to the trial's intensity. And the biggest blessing of all, aside from His Savior Son, is this,

"And we know that for those who love God all things work together for good, for those who are called according to His purpose" (**Rom. 8:28**).

No matter what happens, everything will be okay in the end. The result of all that we have examined and studied so far, the culmination of our obedience and faithfulness to the Shepherd, is this: "we shall dwell in the house of the Lord forever." When we follow our Shepherd to the best grazing while being led along the paths of righteousness, even when things are difficult, a prize awaits us—a prize so beautiful that it is beyond comprehension. That prize is promised to us, along with its inexplicable beauty. **Jam. 1:12** describes the promise:

"Blessed is the man who remains steadfast under trial, for when he has stood the test he will receive the crown of life, which God has promised to those who love him."

So, accept God as your Shepherd; be obedient, fulfilled, led, fed, restored, protected, comforted, victorious, and abundantly blessed for the rest of your life. Secure your dwelling place with the Lord forever.

Chapter 38
Move On or Feel and Stop?

"Now, when Job's three friends heard of all this evil that had come upon him, they came each from his own place, Eliphaz the Temanite, Bildad the Shuhite, and Zophar the Naamathite. They made an appointment together to come to show him sympathy and comfort him. And when they saw him from a distance, they did not recognize him. And they raised their voices and wept, and they tore their robes and sprinkled dust on their heads toward heaven. And they sat with him on the ground seven days and seven nights, and no one spoke a word to him, for they saw that his suffering was very great" (**Job 2:11-13**).

It may seem strange to use Eliphaz, Bildad, and Zophar as examples of true friendship, but hear me out. Even though they didn't offer him sound advice, they were present for him. As you probably know, the unfortunate Job had lost all his livestock, servants, children, and wealth. To make matters worse, he was afflicted with sores that covered his entire body. Those sores were so unbearably itchy and painful that he resorted to using a piece of pottery to scrape his skin. At some point, though we aren't told precisely when, his friends heard about his suffering and decided to visit him.

We are also not told how long that trip took, but we can assume it took weeks since it was not made by plane, train, or vehicle. The journey was likely carried out on the back of a camel, painfully slow, and in the searing heat. Job was a wealthy man who was well-known in the East,

"He possessed 7,000 sheep, 3,000 camels, 500 yoke of oxen, and 500 female donkeys, and very many servants, so that this man was the greatest of all the people of the east" (**Job 1:3**).

It is safe to assume he had many friends, or should I say, acquaintances. You see, only three of all the people he knew took the time to come and comfort him in his hour of need. Were they perfect? Absolutely not, but they still paused their lives to make the trip to see him home.

Good friends may not always provide the best advice or the perfect solution, but they are there to support you in times of need, no matter the discomfort. Acquaintances notice your pain and move on; friends genuinely feel your pain and stay with you. Nowadays, people often collect "friends" like trading cards or something similar. They take pride in their thousands of social media connections, wearing it like a cheap badge of honor. However, if they were ever faced with something even slightly as tragic as what happened to Job, they would quickly discover who their real friends are.

Many years ago, I spent the night in a small town around 400 miles from my hometown. I was driving an 18-wheeler that was giving me trouble, and it would take some time before I could continue my journey. I called home from a payphone to let everyone know it would take a while when I noticed a car pull into the gas station. The car sounded rough, and the driver who got out looked visibly distressed. He needed to use the payphone, so I hung up and let him use it before returning my call. However, I couldn't help but overhear him since I was close by, waiting to use the payphone again.

Almost in tears, he called his friend and told him that circumstances had changed. He could no longer visit him. A couple of hours later, a car pulled in, and a young man jumped out. It was the friend of the guy who was having car trouble. He had traveled 400 miles to pick him up and would take him back, help him fix his car, and then return home. This man would cover 1,600 miles in a week for his friend. That, my friends, is the epitome of true friendship. Job's friends did something similar. When they arrived at his house, they joined him in his grief and remained silent for a week. They did what we all should sometimes do – remain quiet.

In fact, they didn't say a word until he spoke, and that's sound advice. Sometimes, silence is the best response in a given situation. Even when silence isn't the answer, here are a few phrases to avoid: "It will get better soon," "Time heals everything," and "I know how you feel." Time doesn't heal everything; it's a band-aid that can rip off and expose the wound at any moment. They don't want to hear that things will get better soon. Maybe they don't want to hear anything at that moment. Perhaps they just want to sit in silence.

Chapter 39
Hold Fast to the Traditions

"So then, brothers, stand firm and hold to the traditions that you were taught by us, either by our spoken word or by our letter" (**2Th. 2:15**). After discussing the seriousness of the Lord's coming, Paul now provides a concluding exhortation on what the Thessalonian church should do in response. This verse could just as easily apply to thousands of churches today, as many have strayed from sound doctrine. We need only turn on our televisions or browse church apps on our cell phones and tablets to observe how rampant false teaching has become.

In a desperate attempt to grow numerically and financially, church leaders turn to various activities to draw large crowds. Flashy, expensive stage productions and overly loud, in-your-face preaching are designed to appeal to emotions rather than intellect. Motivational speeches, nearly devoid of scripture, assure listeners that God loves them regardless of their actions and that their sins are not their fault. These pastors, along with some self-proclaimed "apostles," spend hours convincing their congregations that unlimited tithing will lead to financial prosperity.

They are told that wealth is merely a prayer away and that their heart's desires only need to be spoken to come true. No ailment will stand against their faith-healing abilities, and life will be one grand "party" if they simply rebuke the devil and drive him away. Their expensive jewelry, clothing, cars, private jets, and mansions contradict their teachings as they enrich themselves at the expense of their congregations. Thousands are invited to the stage to invoke God's eternal blessings by merely confessing Jesus as their Lord and reciting the sinner's prayer.

In other churches, the flock is led astray by teachings that convince them a man can forgive their sins through a series of recitations. They are further taught that the church leader is not Christ, but rather a man with a lofty title and elaborate garments who is presumed to be "infallible" and is referred to as "father," despite the Bible's clear stance teaching. **Mat. 23:9**, "And call no man your father on earth, for you have one Father, who is in heaven." False teachings like these are among the "traditions" made by man rather than derived from the pages of the Bible. Paul urges the church to stand firm and resist the temptation to follow teachings that contradict this gospel. In **Gal. 1:8**, he specifically warns those who are teaching false doctrine:

> "But even if we or an angel from heaven should preach to you a gospel contrary to the one we preached to you, let him be accursed." To the Ephesian elders, the Apostle had this to say, "I know that after my departure fierce wolves will come in among you, not sparing the flock; and from among your own selves will arise men speaking twisted things, to draw away the disciples after them" (**Act. 20:29-30**).

The church should heed his words today and ensure their election by standing firm against false teachers. The church can accomplish this by adhering firmly to the 'traditions' taught by Paul. The traditions he refers to are not mere rituals for self-importance but rather the doctrines entrusted to him. Preaching that lacks scripture and the teachings of the Bible will not secure the church's election or destination. Bible study and sermons should be grounded in the Word rather than in "self-help" books created by men who often have no tolerance for Christianity.

When we treat the church as a place for emotional highs rather than edification, as a source of personal pleasure instead of spiritual enrichment, or where we view ourselves as the sole beneficiaries of the service, we stray from the traditions. The church was never about our feelings but about worshiping God. When we focus on Him rather than ourselves, we will discover that the church can be an encouraging, edifying, and spiritually enriching space. By making church about personal satisfaction, we sow the wrong seeds and risk mocking our Creator, which is never appropriate. **Gal.6:7**, "Do not be deceived: God is not mocked, for whatever one sows, that will he also reap."

Chapter 40
Don't Raise a "Monster"

"Show yourself in all respects to be a model of good works, and in your teaching show integrity, dignity, and sound speech that cannot be condemned, so that an opponent may be put to shame, having nothing evil to say about us" (**Tit. 2:7-8**).

In a chapter that begins with a warning to teach "what accords with sound doctrine," Paul speaks to older men and women about the examples they should set. They are to conduct themselves in a certain way to teach and raise sound men and women of God, and this lesson similarly applies to us today.

Addressing each group individually while applying the criteria to both, Paul includes the following: "...sober-minded, dignified, self-controlled, sound in faith, in love, and steadfastness... reverent in behavior, not slanderers or slaves to much wine" (**Tit 2:2-3**). Of course, these are not the only qualities mature individuals should exhibit when mentoring younger people, but they summarize traits that promote effective mentoring teaching. In **v. 5**, the following are added, "...be self-controlled, pure, working at home, kind, and submissive to their own husbands..."

The third and fifth verses may have been explicitly directed at women, but it can't be denied that the rest also apply to men. Men are not exempt from demonstrating self-control or kindness just because they are men. In fact, in the very next verse, Paul instructs his readers to urge "younger men to be self-controlled." What Paul means is that you cannot expect to be successful in teaching others if you are not willing to apply those lessons to yourself first. When we were preteens, my father caught my sister smoking a cigarette. As punishment, he made her smoke several in a row until she felt sick—then went and smoked one himself. I've always thought that was a strange lesson—to expect her not to do something he did himself time.

A smoker cannot effectively teach the dangers of smoking, a liar cannot instill honesty, an adulterer cannot inspire faithfulness, a violent person cannot teach restraint, and a prideful individual cannot model humility—not while persisting in those vices. I once heard an adult use profanity in front of a child and then be called out by the child. The parent, clearly annoyed at the child's 'rudeness,' responded, "Mommy is using 'grown-up' words. Grown-ups can use them, but kids cannot. You have your own words. If you use mine, I will punish you... do you hear me?"

The same parent would later say, "You need to follow my example if you want to be a 'proper' grown-up one day." Well, she was trying to follow her mother's example, wasn't she? That perfectly illustrates the phrase, "Do as I say, not as I do." Paul directly addresses that fallacy with the words, "Show yourself in all respects to be a model of good works." Be what you want them to be. Sober-minded adults understand that their actions are imitated more than their words alone. This is no different in the church. In fact, it could be argued that it is even more important. How absolutely shocking is it to see individuals preach what they do not apply to themselves?

Raising strong leaders in the church is already challenging because of worldly influences on young, impressionable minds—why make it even harder? Furthermore, failing to practice what we preach exposes both ourselves and the church to ridicule. This will happen if you are double-minded in your words and actions. Always remember, the future of our youth is in your hands. Don't raise a "monster" and then cry when it acts like one. **Pro. 22:6**, "Train up a child in the way he should go; even when he is old he will not depart from it."

Chapter 41
No Longer the Moral Compass

> "Now the works of the flesh are evident: sexual immorality, impurity, sensuality, idolatry, sorcery, enmity, strife, jealousy, fits of anger, rivalries, dissensions, divisions, envy, drunkenness, orgies, and things like these. I warn you, as I warned you before, that those who do such things will not inherit the kingdom of God" (**Gal. 5:19-21**).

Few would disagree with me when I say that the world appears to have lost its moral compass. Of course, I'm not claiming that all the sins Paul mentions in today's passage are new—they're not. What I'm saying is that our moral compass must be guided by God's teachings, not man's.

The church is responsible for mirroring those teachings and being the moral compass for society. **Ecc. 1:9-10**,

> "What has been is what will be, and what has been done is what will be done, and there is nothing new under the sun. Is there a thing of which it is said, "See, this is new"? It has been already in the ages before us."

Clearly, then, the issues we face have been encountered before. Nonetheless, I assert that we are currently in a time when the overwhelming presence of insidious ideologies has put us in a spiritually precarious position. Many law-abiding Christians are genuinely concerned about the country's direction and, indeed, the world.

The church faces unprecedented social pressures in our lifetimes, and the temptation to 'go along with it for the sake of peace' is significant. Take abortion, for example. The fact that the church considers infanticide a sin should not come as a surprise. Some who support it, including certain Christ-professing groups, cite **Exo. 21:22-25**,

"When men strive together and hit a pregnant woman, so that her children come out, but there is no harm, the one who hit her shall surely be fined, as the woman's husband shall impose on him, and he shall pay as the judges determine. But if there is harm, then you shall pay life for life, eye for eye, tooth for tooth, hand for hand, foot for foot, burn for burn, wound for wound, stripe for stripe."

Of course, citing that while ignoring **Jer. 1:5** is misguided: "Before I formed you in the womb I knew you, and before you were born I consecrated you; I appointed you a prophet to the nations."

If God knows every person before they are born, it stands to reason that He has brought them into being and serves as the sole arbiter of life and death. However, even using the Exodus verses to support abortion is, at best, a stretch. The interpretation must be twisted for anyone to believe that miscarriage is being addressed. Significantly, there is forgiveness available for sins that are genuinely repented. God is a loving, merciful, and forgiving being, after all.

Next, let's examine the recent trend regarding gender dysphoria. There are now tens, if not hundreds, of recognized genders, with supporters claiming that the gender assigned by a doctor at birth may not correspond with an individual's self-identification. In other words, someone identified as male at birth may later identify as female or another gender at any stage of their life. Furthermore, this trend allows such individuals to use female restrooms and showers and to compete in female athletic events. In fact, one politician recently became outraged when an opponent made the "shocking" claim that only women can get pregnant.

Once again, the Bible provides clear guidance on the issue of gender. **Gen. 1:27**, "So God created man in his own image, in the image of God he created him; male and female he created them." The third issue I want to address is same-sex marriage. Homosexuality is not a new phenomenon, but that doesn't mean the Bible condones it. In fact, passages in the Old and New Testaments expressly forbid it. **Rom. 1:26-27**,

"For this reason God gave them up to dishonorable passions. For their women exchanged natural relations for those that are contrary to nature; and the men likewise gave up natural relations with women and were consumed with passion for one another...."

The pervasiveness of these 'modern' trends inevitably brings to mind the story of Sodom and Gomorrah. Does this mean there should be no love for people? Absolutely not, unless one removes **Mat. 22:37-40** from the Bible, but it also does not mean Christians must agree with their choices. When the church seeks moral direction from man instead of God out of fear of ostracism or attack, it forfeits its role as the world's moral compass. We are called to love every person, and they have the God-given right to accept or reject His teachings. However, this does not mean the church must compromise its beliefs to align with political correctness. Love and disagreement can coexist. Love must prevail despite differences.

Chapter 42
The Old vs. The New

"For whatever was written in former days was written for our instruction, that through endurance and through the encouragement of the Scriptures we might have hope" (**Rom. 15:4**).

I want to address a comment a reader made to me yesterday. Essentially, he stated that the Old Testament is not relevant today. I usually don't answer posts because I receive hundreds of comments on various platforms and pages, but I noticed this one and decided to respond. I am not trying to embarrass anyone, but I believe the conversation we had, though brief, has value.

First, let me say this: I enjoy debating someone who has a different view of scripture than I do. We can all learn from those conversations or debates, and I am not arrogant enough to think that I am beyond misunderstanding something. That said, let me continue. I replied by referencing **Rom. 15:4**, thinking it would address his concern so we could move on, but that was not the case. The gentleman responded by quoting **Deu. 25:11-12**,

> "When men fight with one another, and the wife of the one draws near to rescue her husband from the hand of him who is beating him and puts out her hand and seizes him by the private parts, then you shall cut off her hand. Your eye shall have no pity."

I am not confused about the value of the two Testaments. I am a New Testament Christian and live by the teachings of Jesus and the epistles: **Col. 2:14**, "...by canceling the record of debt that stood against us with its legal demands. This he set aside, nailing it to the cross." I understand what the sacrifice of Christ on the cross meant, and I am good with that: **Heb. 8:13**, "In speaking of a new covenant, he makes the first one obsolete. And what is becoming obsolete and growing old is ready to vanish away." Again, I understand and accept that His work on the cross removed the convoluted laws and restrictions.

However, embracing the New Testament teachings while disregarding the Old Testament's lessons is short-sighted. Consider how **Pro. 3:5-6** remains a lesson for us today: "Trust in the Lord with all your heart, and do not lean on your own understanding. In all your ways acknowledge him, and he will make straight your paths." Also, consider how the story of David and Bathsheba remains relevant today. Adultery was as wrong then as it is now, so there is value in studying that story. There are countless lessons we can learn from the Old Testament.

This was my response to his second comment: "There is tremendous value in studying the Old Testament. When I was young, my father drank a lot. I learned not to drink and passed that on to my sons as well. Negative history lessons can lead to positive future behavior. Of course, history has valuable lessons; otherwise, we would still have slaves, etc." There is a vast difference between following laws and learning from past mistakes and successes. If the Old Testament were just a historical footnote, why would it have been included in the canon? And why would Paul even say the words of **Rom. 15:4**? Moreover, anyone who has studied the New Testament will recognize how often its authors referenced or quoted the Old Testament.

I trust my answer has satisfied the reader, and he will recognize the value of not strictly adhering to all those cumbersome laws but learning valuable lessons from our forefathers. As the well-known saying goes, "Those who fail to learn from history are doomed to repeat it." How can we avoid repeating those mistakes if we never study them? We stand on the shoulders of the faithful of the past and should embrace all we can learn from them.

Chapter 43
Beatitude (pt. 1) The Poor in Spirit

"Blessed are the poor in spirit, for theirs is the kingdom of heaven. "Blessed are those who mourn, for they shall be comforted. "Blessed are the meek, for they shall inherit the earth. "Blessed are those who hunger and thirst for righteousness, for they shall be satisfied. "Blessed are the merciful, for they shall receive mercy. "Blessed are the pure in heart, for they shall see God.

"Blessed are the peacemakers, for they shall be called sons of God. "Blessed are those who are persecuted for righteousness' sake, for theirs is the kingdom of heaven. "Blessed are you when others revile you and persecute you and utter all kinds of evil against you falsely on my account. Rejoice and be glad, for your reward is great in heaven, for so they persecuted the prophets who were before you" (**Mat. 5:3-12**).

Today, we are examining the first beatitude: "Blessed are the poor in spirit, for theirs is the kingdom of heaven." Many believe Jesus is speaking to the materially poor because "in the spirit" is left out in **Luk. 6:20**, "Blessed are you who are poor, for yours is the kingdom of God," but careful hermeneutics prove otherwise. When passages seem contradictory, best practice dictates that the clearer one should be chosen. This does not imply that there is no parallel between financial poverty and those who are poor in spirit, but in this instance, Jesus addresses spiritual poverty.

Let me explain it this way. If Jesus were actually saying that those who are financially poor are blessed while excluding the rich, it would have profound implications. First, by excluding the wealthy, He would be suggesting that they would never be blessed and could not enter the Kingdom of Heaven. While Jesus mentions that it is hard for them to do so because of the distractions that wealth can bring, He also states that anything is possible with God: **Mat. 19:23-24, 26,**

"And Jesus said to his disciples, "Truly, I say to you, only with difficulty will a rich person enter the kingdom of heaven. Again, I tell you, it is easier for a camel to go through the eye of a needle than for a rich person to enter the kingdom of God...**26**, "With man this is impossible, but with God all things are possible."

The poor do have an advantage because they are not distracted by "toys," "arrogance," or "pride," but to say only they are blessed and will enter the kingdom of heaven is incorrect. There were rich men in the Bible who died blessed. Job was wealthy. "And the Lord blessed the latter days of Job more than his beginning. And he had 14,000 sheep, 6,000 camels, 1,000 yoke of oxen, and 1,000 female donkeys" (**Job 42:12**). Solomon was staggeringly rich: **2 Chr. 9:22**, "Thus King Solomon excelled all the kings of the earth in riches and in wisdom." Job and King Solomon were among the many wealthy and blessed individuals mentioned in the Bible, so being rich is not necessarily bad.

Having an abundance comes with certain selfish dangers, but it is not an automatic condemnation. **Deut.15:11**, "For there will never cease to be poor in the land. Therefore, I command you, 'You shall open wide your hand to your brother, to the needy and to the poor, in your land." Note that the scripture above does not condemn the rich but instructs them to help those in need. **1Jo. 3:17**, "But if anyone has the world's goods and sees his brother in need, yet closes his heart against him, how does God's love abide in him?" Our Christian duty is to help those in need, but if we ignore this and instead hoard treasures for ourselves on earth, we risk condemnation. (**Luk. 16:19-31**).

The second implication is that poverty is a necessary condition for salvation, but the Bible clearly does not teach this. If only the poor were blessed, God would urge us to give up everything we have and live in extreme financial need to be saved. We would also find no instruction to assist those in need, as their current situation guarantees them blessings and entry into heaven. An important lesson from this reading is that neither the rich nor the poor can earn salvation on their own. Both need Christ, without whom neither has any hope.

Chapter 44
Beatitudes (pt. 2) The Poor in Spirit

"Blessed are the poor in spirit, for theirs is the kingdom of heaven. "Blessed are those who mourn, for they shall be comforted. "Blessed are the meek, for they shall inherit the earth. "Blessed are those who hunger and thirst for righteousness, for they shall be satisfied. "Blessed are the merciful, for they shall receive mercy. "Blessed are the pure in heart, for they shall see God.

"Blessed are the peacemakers, for they shall be called sons of God. "Blessed are those who are persecuted for righteousness' sake, for theirs is the kingdom of heaven. "Blessed are you when others revile you and persecute you and utter all kinds of evil against you falsely on my account. Rejoice and be glad, for your reward is great in heaven, for so they persecuted the prophets who were before you" (**Mat. 5:3-12**).

Yesterday, we concluded that the author was not referring to those who are financially poor but to those who are spiritually poor. I believe the simplest way to explain what "poor in spirit" means is to interpret it as "those who are humble." The wealthy are often prideful and arrogant, lacking humility, while the needy typically embody it. Prideful and arrogant individuals abandon their spiritual dependency and rely solely on themselves, whereas the humble, who are poor in spirit, acknowledge their dependence on God. When we depend on Him for our needs, we will better understand His role in our lives and remain faithful and obedient to Him.

God rejects the prideful and accepts the humble. **Jam. 4:6**, "...Therefore it says, "God opposes the proud but gives grace to the humble." God knows the mind of man fully, understanding our every weakness. He knows who will stay obedient and who will decide to "go it alone." The subject of humility is so important that Peter uses the same words himself. **1Pe. 5:5**, "Likewise, you who are younger, be subject to the elders. Clothe yourselves, all of you, with humility toward one another, for "God opposes the proud but gives grace to the humble."

Here, we clearly see the connection between obedience and humility.

Peter then connects those two characteristics in the following verse. **1Pe. 5:6**, "Humble yourselves, therefore, under the mighty hand of God so that at the proper time he may exalt you." The humble recognize their position before God and express gratitude for His guidance in their lives. And, in turn, God will "exalt" them, which is the blessing of being raised up by the grace He showers the poor in spirit with. God has always had a heart for the humble. **Isa. 57:15**, "...I dwell in the high and holy place, and also with him who is of a contrite and lowly spirit, to revive the spirit of the lowly, and to revive the heart of the contrite." Who is of a "contrite and lowly spirit" if not those who are "poor in spirit."

Poverty in spirit can be viewed as the key to salvation because it will rely on the Creator for the roadmap to heaven. In response to the question of "Who is the greatest in the kingdom of heaven," Jesus has this to say in **Mat. 18:1-4**, "...And calling to him a child, he put him in the midst of them and said, 'Truly, I say to you, unless you turn and become like children, you will never enter the kingdom of heaven. Whoever humbles himself like this child is the greatest in the kingdom of heaven.'"

Children depend on parents or guardians for everything, and they recognize that. Their humility and lack of pride are two of their greatest assets of youth.

We should treasure those assets as well. Jesus shared another important truth: the humble have a special blessing awaiting them. They deserve this blessing because, through humility, they can resist the devil and draw near to God, understanding that in His arms is everything they need. If you are not humble, stop believing you have all the answers. You may seem to have it all together with your wealth and prideful arrogance, but the illusions of the world will vanish instantly, leaving you without blessings in a place of torment.

Chapter 45
Beatitudes (pt. 3) Those Who Mourn

"Blessed are the poor in spirit, for theirs is the kingdom of heaven. "Blessed are those who mourn, for they shall be comforted. "Blessed are the meek, for they shall inherit the earth. "Blessed are those who hunger and thirst for righteousness, for they shall be satisfied. "Blessed are the merciful, for they shall receive mercy. "Blessed are the pure in heart, for they shall see God.

"Blessed are the peacemakers, for they shall be called sons of God. "Blessed are those who are persecuted for righteousness' sake, for theirs is the kingdom of heaven. "Blessed are you when others revile you and persecute you and utter all kinds of evil against you falsely on my account. Rejoice and be glad, for your reward is great in heaven, for so they persecuted the prophets who were before you" (**Mat 5:3-12**).

As we continue our study of the beatitudes, we will examine the phrase, "Blessed are those who mourn, for they shall be comforted." Many readers interpret these words as referring to someone who has lost a loved one. While this interpretation can certainly provide great comfort, the author intends a different meaning. There are two perspectives on Matthew's message. The first argues that he speaks of those who "mourn" due to persecution and poverty. The second refers to those who "mourn" because of the sorrow and guilt of sin. Rather than selecting one viewpoint, it is helpful to see it as encompassing both interpretations while also extending comfort to those grieving the loss of a loved one.

Some refer to **Luk. 6:21** as a parallel and evidence supporting the idea that Matthew is addressing personal bereavement: "Blessed are you who are hungry now, for you shall be satisfied. "Blessed are you who weep now, for you shall laugh." The dualistic nature of scripture undoubtedly allows for such interpretations; however, Luke's approach is more literal, while Matthew's is more spiritual. Additionally, Luke's passage specifically addresses the disciples and their material and social disadvantages, whereas Matthew's audience is much broader. Once again, the interpretation is more fluid than simply 'this or that,' but understanding its true intent is essential to fully appreciating the depth of the blessing.

You will notice a theme if you read through the selected verses. Matthew commends those whom the world typically looks down on or rejects, assigning them a value that transcends this world. How comforting it is to know that there is a reward for those who are undervalued because of their spiritual compass. Isaiah addresses this to those who endure hardship in this world. **Isa. 61:1-3**,

> "The Spirit of the Lord God is upon me, because the Lord has anointed me to bring good news to the poor; he has sent me to bind up the brokenhearted, to proclaim liberty to the captives, and the opening of the prison to those who are bound; to proclaim the year of the Lord 's favor, and the day of vengeance of our God; to comfort all who mourn; to grant to those who mourn in Zion— to give them a beautiful headdress instead of ashes, the oil of gladness instead of mourning, the garment of praise instead of a faint spirit; that they may be called oaks of righteousness, the planting of the Lord, that he may be glorified."

I especially love the verses above because they elevate those who mourn to a place of honor and favor in God's sight. Their current circumstances do not define their future happiness. They will be adorned in the beauty of God's glory and stand righteous before Him. What beautiful words for all who mourn, regardless of the reason. No matter your personal struggles, God is always close, ready to comfort and restore you.

Chapter 46
Beatitudes (pt. 4) The Meek

"Blessed are the poor in spirit, for theirs is the kingdom of heaven. "Blessed are those who mourn, for they shall be comforted. "Blessed are the meek, for they shall inherit the earth. "Blessed are those who hunger and thirst for righteousness, for they shall be satisfied. "Blessed are the merciful, for they shall receive mercy. "Blessed are the pure in heart, for they shall see God.

"Blessed are the peacemakers, for they shall be called sons of God. "Blessed are those who are persecuted for righteousness' sake, for theirs is the kingdom of heaven. "Blessed are you when others revile you and persecute you and utter all kinds of evil against you falsely on my account. Rejoice and be glad, for your reward is great in heaven, for so they persecuted the prophets who were before you" (**Mat. 5:3-12**).

Today, we will focus on the beatitude, "Blessed are the meek, for they shall inherit the earth." The word "meek" is defined as "patient and mild; not inclined to anger or resentment." It also includes humility, a trait found in those who are poor in spirit and mourn. We will discover that the best spiritual characteristics are found in all whom the Beatitudes speak of and call Christians to be like. If you are striving to be meek, it is crucial to remember this: "Meekness is not the same as weakness." The world will define anyone who displays that noble characteristic as a pathetic, weak individual to be scoffed at and scorned.

Someone used the analogy of a bridled horse as an example of meekness. With a bit and bridle, the horse chooses to be under the rider's authority. It is "power under constraint." It is being able to but choosing not to act in a specific situation. One could say that the meek are slow to anger, a quality the Bible encourages. **Jam. 1:19-20** says,

"Know this, my beloved brothers: let every person be quick to hear, slow to speak, slow to anger; for the anger of man does not produce the righteousness of God."

The third beatitude highlights an important strength to develop: the ability to think before acting, whether in words or actions. But the world cares little for that. It wants you to overreact – to show strength in active response.

It encourages you to show power through arrogance and to destroy anyone who opposes you, urging an active, aggressive response. The Bible encourages meekness, the act of passively resisting an attack by showing patient restraint. The down-to-earth, modest person does not have to prove who they are by their unrestraint. Their power is displayed not in violence but in the strength of silence. To walk away from a fight is not cowardice; it is courageous meekness, for which you will be rewarded richly in the future. In Titus, we find the perfect example of what it means to be meek. **Tit. 3:2**, "...to speak evil of no one, to avoid quarreling, to be gentle, and to show perfect courtesy toward all people."

In **Psa. 37:11**, we read words that are very similar to today's beatitude. However, back up one verse to **Psa. 37:10**, and the plight of the arrogant is revealed,

"In just a little while, the wicked will be no more; though you look carefully at his place, he will not be there. But the meek shall inherit the land and delight themselves in abundant peace."

While **v. 11** specifically refers to the Abrahamic land promise, it also signifies that God thoroughly blessed them—a blessing that applies to **Mat. 5:5** as well. I view it as being rewarded with a suitable measure of blessings on earth, leading to the ultimate reward of eternity in heaven. If you want your allotted share of blessings and the fulfillment of God's promise to be forever with Him, practice meekness.

Chapter 47
Beatitudes (pt. 5) Hunger and Thirst

"Blessed are the poor in spirit, for theirs is the kingdom of heaven. "Blessed are those who mourn, for they shall be comforted. "Blessed are the meek, for they shall inherit the earth. "Blessed are those who hunger and thirst for righteousness, for they shall be satisfied. "Blessed are the merciful, for they shall receive mercy. "Blessed are the pure in heart, for they shall see God.

"Blessed are the peacemakers, for they shall be called sons of God. "Blessed are those who are persecuted for righteousness' sake, for theirs is the kingdom of heaven. "Blessed are you when others revile you and persecute you and utter all kinds of evil against you falsely on my account. Rejoice and be glad, for your reward is great in heaven, for so they persecuted the prophets who were before you" (**Mat. 5:3-12**).

Today, we will examine the fifth beatitude: "Blessed are those who hunger and thirst for righteousness, for they shall be satisfied." Most of us have experienced hunger to one degree or another. It happens to us every day. At some point, we begin to experience hunger pangs – a message from our body to remind us we need sustenance. We go to the kitchen, store, or vending machine and quickly prepare or purchase a snack before moving on with our day. However, if we cannot find food, the initial discomfort we experience can become much more serious. We may begin to feel weak and tired, with our motor functions slowing down noticeably. We become lethargic and, at some point, a little desperate.

When you are thirsty, the problem becomes more severe, much sooner. Whereas an adult can live up to 70 days without food, it will only take three to four days to kill someone who cannot drink water. When you are thirsty enough, you will get a headache and feel dizzy, and the desire to drink will become an obsession. Instinctively, your body knows how critical water is, and you will do almost anything to drink some. The drive to drink water can be so strong that some have even drunk seawater in desperation, resulting in severe illness or death.

In the spiritual sense, the hunger and thirst for righteousness represent the soul seeking God. **Ecc. 3:11**, "He has made everything beautiful in its time. Also, he has put eternity into man's heart...." The human condition is a fallen state, but despite that, every individual has a craving that needs to be satisfied – God. Some do not believe this and instead, turn to worldly pursuits to fill their desperate need for fulfillment. They will gorge themselves on the world's delights in a vain attempt to be satisfied. Money, drugs, sex, fame, and power are but a few of the things they will consume to fill the void, but none of them will satisfy the intense hunger and thirst. The more they grab and feast on them, the more the inexplicable hunger and thirst will increase.

They fail to realize that what they need most is the very thing they refuse to accept. The words of **Psa. 41:1-2** has been turned into a beautiful hymn. We have all sung it in church, and most of us love it. It has a message that speaks directly to our lesson today. "As a deer pants for flowing streams, so pants my soul for you, O God. My soul thirsts for God, for the living God...." Our souls search for God, yet our stubborn hearts often prevent us from finding spiritual nourishment in Him. Jesus also told the Samaritan woman at the well, **Joh. 4:14**, "...but whoever drinks of the water that I will give him will never be thirsty again. The water that I will give him will become in him a spring of water welling up to eternal life."

Our Savior says those who hunger and thirst for righteousness are blessed, and they are because they will find the nourishment for their souls in Him – if they seek Him. They view the things of God as spiritual necessities and are 'desperate' to partake of them. This becomes their highest priority, and they are richly rewarded for their efforts. They will be spiritually, emotionally, and psychologically satisfied and can look forward to a better forever. Are you hungry and thirsty for righteousness? Will you turn to the World or to the Word to satisfy that innate craving?

Chapter 48
Beatitudes (pt. 6) The Merciful

"Blessed are the poor in spirit, for theirs is the kingdom of heaven. "Blessed are those who mourn, for they shall be comforted. "Blessed are the meek, for they shall inherit the earth. "Blessed are those who hunger and thirst for righteousness, for they shall be satisfied. "Blessed are the merciful, for they shall receive mercy.

"Blessed are the pure in heart, for they shall see God.

"Blessed are the peacemakers, for they shall be called sons of God. "Blessed are those who are persecuted for righteousness' sake, for theirs is the kingdom of heaven. "Blessed are you when others revile you and persecute you and utter all kinds of evil against you falsely on my account. Rejoice and be glad, for your reward is great in heaven, for so they persecuted the prophets who were before you" (**Mat. 5:3-12**).

Today, as we continue our study of the Beatitudes, we will examine the sixth one: "Blessed are the merciful, for they shall receive mercy." The first four Beatitudes focus on God, but now the emphasis shifts to actions that reflect righteous living. Who exactly are the merciful spoken of in today's lesson? The scholar Erasmus described them as follows, "... those who, through brotherly love, account another person's misery their own; who weep over the calamities of others; who, out of their property, feed the hungry and clothe the naked; who admonish those that are in error, inform the ignorant, pardon the offending; and who, in short, use their utmost endeavors to relieve and comfort others."

Merciful people have the ability to empathize with others. They are able to "understand and share the feelings of another." They have another fundamental trait as well – love. No one who lacks love for their fellow man is merciful. A perfect example of an unmerciful person—and the consequences they face—is found in **Mat. 18:21-35**. Peter asked the Lord how often he should forgive a brother who sinned against him, prompting Jesus to share the parable of the unforgiving servant. A servant who owed a king ten thousand talents was ordered to be sold along with his wife, children, and all he had, but after pleading for mercy, the king relented and forgave him. Soon after that, however, he would not show a fellow slave the same mercy for a debt owed.

After choking him, the unforgiving servant had him thrown in jail. When the king heard that he had shown no mercy, he was imprisoned until he could repay the debt. The parable ends with these words, "So also my heavenly Father will do to every one of you, if you do not forgive your brother from your heart" (**Mat. 18:35**). Show no mercy, and none will be shown to you. Do not be deceived into thinking you do not need mercy yourself. You are a sinner and will need every ounce of mercy available to you. Instead of being "that" person, try emulating your God and Father. **Psa. 18:25**, "With the merciful you show yourself merciful; with the blameless man you show yourself blameless."

When the Pharisees asked why Jesus was sitting with sinners and tax collectors, He replied with the following words,

> "Those who are well have no need of a physician, but those who are sick. Go and learn what this means: 'I desire mercy and not sacrifice.' For I came not to call the righteous, but sinners" (**Mat. 9:13**).

Learn what it means that Jesus desires mercy. Understand that mercy involves forgiving others, empathizing with the plight of the poor, feeding the hungry, and clothing the naked. But that is not all; the merciful will correct the errant soul because of their love for that individual. They will teach and direct the lost person out of the darkness of sin into the loving, merciful light of Jesus Christ.

God is a God of mercy, but He is also a fair and righteous judge who will not shower it on those unwilling to show mercy to someone else. We should strive not to be like the merciless, for they will receive none in return. **Jam. 2:13**, "For judgment is without mercy to one who has shown no mercy. Mercy triumphs over judgment."

Chapter 49
Beatitude (pt. 7) The Pure in Heart

"Blessed are the poor in spirit, for theirs is the kingdom of heaven. "Blessed are those who mourn, for they shall be comforted. "Blessed are the meek, for they shall inherit the earth. "Blessed are those who hunger and thirst for righteousness, for they shall be satisfied. "Blessed are the merciful, for they shall receive mercy. "Blessed are the pure in heart, for they shall see God.

"Blessed are the peacemakers, for they shall be called sons of God. "Blessed are those who are persecuted for righteousness' sake, for theirs is the kingdom of heaven. "Blessed are you when others revile you and persecute you and utter all kinds of evil against you falsely on my account. Rejoice and be glad, for your reward is great in heaven, for so they persecuted the prophets who were before you" (**Mat. 5:3-12**).

Today, we will examine the beatitude, "Blessed are the pure in heart, for they shall see God." Only those who are pure in heart "shall see God." **Psa. 24:3-4**,

> "Who shall ascend the hill of the Lord? And who shall stand in his holy place? He who has clean hands and a pure heart, who does not lift up his soul to what is false and does not swear deceitfully."

By contrast, those who are not pure in heart will have a problem on the Day of Judgment.
They may think they fool everyone. They may even believe they can fool God, but this is a grave mistake with eternal consequences. They will reap the actions of their heart. God will test us and find us either satisfactory or lacking. He can search the farthest depths of our hearts, and His righteous judgment will follow from that, "I the Lord search the heart and test the mind, to give every man according to his ways, according to the fruit of his deeds" (**Jer. 17:10**). Sadly, they may even think they are right. They may live

their lives believing they are saved, convinced their actions please God and will be rewarded.

But once again, they are wrong and will be rudely awakened. **Pro. 21:2**, "Every way of a man is right in his own eyes, but the Lord weighs the heart." When you act in ways contrary to the Bible, you are the antithesis of pure in heart. If your actions are driven by malice, if you willfully intend to cause harm, or if you are dishonest, disobedient, and disloyal to God, you are not pure in heart. You should then examine yourself honestly and strive to change yourself before it is too late – even if you are a Christian. **Mat. 7:21**, "Not everyone who says to me, 'Lord, Lord,' will enter the kingdom of heaven, but the one who does the will of my Father who is in heaven."

However, if you are pure in heart, your eternal destination will be more beautiful than you can imagine. **1Co.2:9**, "What no eye has seen, nor ear heard, nor the heart of man imagined, what God has prepared for those who love him." Having inner moral integrity is the hallmark of someone who will "see God." It is not hard to be someone like that. After all, we have a manual that tells us exactly how to achieve and maintain a pure heart. But, if it seems too difficult, we can turn to the author of the Bible for help. **Psa. 51:10**, "Create in me a clean heart, O God, and renew a right spirit within me."

Mankind is fallen, and attempting to be pure in heart without God's help is like trying to fly a kite on a windless day—a futile endeavor. You can run around as fast as you can, but your efforts will only see the kite rise a few feet before crashing to the ground repeatedly. Eventually, you will grow weary and give up. Just as a kite needs wind to soar, you need God's help through the Holy Spirit, who dwells in baptized believers, to cultivate a pure heart.

Your eternal destination will then be the glorious place we call heaven. Then, you will see God – not for a day, a week, a month, or a year, but for all eternity. Imagine being in the presence of our Creator, whose magnificence is beyond human grasp.

Chapter 50
Beatitudes (pt. 8) The Peacemakers

"Blessed are the poor in spirit, for theirs is the kingdom of heaven. "Blessed are those who mourn, for they shall be comforted. "Blessed are the meek, for they shall inherit the earth. "Blessed are those who hunger and thirst for righteousness, for they shall be satisfied. "Blessed are the merciful, for they shall receive mercy. "Blessed are the pure in heart, for they shall see God'

"Blessed are the peacemakers, for they shall be called sons of God. "Blessed are those who are persecuted for righteousness' sake, for theirs is the kingdom of heaven. "Blessed are you when others revile you and persecute you and utter all kinds of evil against you falsely on my account. Rejoice and be glad, for your reward is great in heaven, for so they persecuted the prophets who were before you" (**Mat. 5:3-12**).

As we continue exploring the meaning of the beatitudes, we will focus on, "Blessed are the peacemakers, for they shall be called sons of God." Have you ever found yourself in a situation with a family member or friend where a minor disagreement escalated to the point of damaging the relationship? Eye contact is avoided, and sitting on the same side of the church is no longer an option. Friends feel compelled to choose sides, and both parties often view those who remain neutral as traitors. Not everyone desires peace. Some allow a disagreement to fester into resentment, and uncontrolled resentment will lead to hatred. Along the way, family bonds or friendships are lost to pride, and unresolved anger and unhappiness morph into a desire for revenge.

Over the years, I have learned to walk away from conflicts driven by emotional outbursts fueled by anger. It takes a long time to develop the ability to do so because we have an innate desire to match anger with anger. We do not want to appear weaker, or our desire to be heard leads us to act in kind. The result is that no empathy is felt, and little is heard as we try to force our opinion on the other person without regard to the damage we could be causing to the relationship. It goes without saying that one could hardly be called a peacemaker in that situation.

Jesus wants us to be different from the world, to undress ourselves of the spirit of anger and retaliation, and to put on the spirit of peace. Remaining calm when someone else has 'lost it' can be difficult but often saves relationships. Only by learning to do that personally can you be a peacemaker for others. The church needs individuals who are gifted with the ability to remain unbiased, calm, and peaceable. When two people are in conflict, often the only thing that can resolve their differences is an arbiter. If the parties involved in the dispute are willing to set aside their emotionally driven anger, they will listen to the words of the mediator and save their relationship.

An effective arbiter has the spirit of reconciliation. We need to look no further than Jesus Himself to find the perfect example of that spirit. **Eph. 2:14-17**,

> "For he himself is our peace, who has made us both one and has broken down in his flesh the dividing wall of hostility by abolishing the law of commandments expressed in ordinances, that he might create in himself one new man in place of the two, so making peace, and might reconcile us both to God in one body through the cross, thereby killing the hostility. And he came and preached peace to you who were far off and peace to those who were near."

Thankfully, we do not need to sacrifice ourselves to reconcile the two parties. We must remain unbiased and consider both parties' views with love and respect. Then, we can advise them on the best, Godly solution. Consider being a peacemaker from this day forward.

Chapter 51
Beatitudes (pt. 9) Persecuted

"Blessed are the poor in spirit, for theirs is the kingdom of heaven. "Blessed are those who mourn, for they shall be comforted. "Blessed are the meek, for they shall inherit the earth. "Blessed are those who hunger and thirst for righteousness, for they shall be satisfied. "Blessed are the merciful, for they shall receive mercy.

"Blessed are the pure in heart, for they shall see God.

"Blessed are the peacemakers, for they shall be called sons of God. "Blessed are those who are persecuted for righteousness' sake, for theirs is the kingdom of heaven. "Blessed are you when others revile you and persecute you and utter all kinds of evil against you falsely on my account. Rejoice and be glad, for your reward is great in heaven, for so they persecuted the prophets who were before you" (**Mat. 5:3-12**).

Today, we will look at the final beatitude:

> "Blessed are those who are persecuted for righteousness' sake, for theirs is the kingdom of heaven. Blessed are you when others revile you and persecute you and utter all kinds of evil against you falsely on my account. Rejoice and be glad, for your reward is great in heaven, for so they persecuted the prophets who were before you."

The definition of persecution in the above context is "hostility and ill-treatment because of religious beliefs." This action against Christians is unwarranted and represents a form of bias and prejudice based on our beliefs. If we choose to associate with office gossip or with divisive, angry individuals, we may face hostility from our co-workers, but that is to be expected. In a sense, we hang a noose of persecution around our necks and should anticipate nothing less. However, Jesus is not speaking of that type of association. He states, "...for righteousness' sake." If we suffer for His sake, we should expect hostility and mistreatment, but not because it would be justified in this case. John explains it with the words of Jesus in **Joh. 15:18-20**,

> "If the world hates you, know that it has hated me before it hated you. If you were of the world, the world would love you as its own; but because you are not of the world, but I chose you out of the world, therefore the world hates you. Remember the word that I said to you: 'A servant is not greater than his master.' If they persecuted me, they will also persecute you....."

Jesus says the world will persecute us because He chose us out of the world and that we should expect nothing less. He also says they will do so on account of His name because they do not know God. The world discriminates against us and disparages us because we align ourselves with the teachings of God rather than man. Even though King Darius' advisors convinced him to decree that any person who worships a god other than him would be thrown into the lion's den, Daniel still worshipped his God (**Dan. 6**). Even the threat of death could not deter him from worshiping his Creator, and he willingly faced persecution for that choice. If only we could possess such immense resolve ourselves in the face of the verbal or emotional abuse we endure as Christians.

> In **Act. 6**, some in the synagogue "could not withstand the wisdom and the Spirit with which he was speaking" (**v10**) and "set up false witnesses against him" (**v. 13**). This man, who performed great signs and wonders for the Kingdom's cause, was attacked for his beliefs and stoned—something Saul approved of. Of course, those are not the only stories, but they are indicative of the worst kinds of persecution believers can face. I would be remiss not to mention our Lord Jesus and the example of His steadfastness despite the persecution and suffering He endured. His example should be our motivation – the determination to survive no matter the cost. **1Pe. 2:20-21**, "For what credit is it if, when you

sin and are beaten for it, you endure? But if when you do good and suffer for it you endure, this is a gracious thing in the sight of God. For to this you have been called, because Christ also suffered for you, leaving you an example, so that you might follow in his steps."

If you must endure suffering, ensure it is for righteousness' sake. You are not alone; you are not the first to suffer persecution, and you certainly won't be the last. Jesus says to rejoice because your reward will be great in heaven—and who wouldn't want that reward?

Chapter 52
What Does Your Heart Reflect?

"Even a child makes himself known by his acts, by whether his conduct is pure and upright" (**Pro. 20:11**). Many people wear a figurative mask in public. They behave in a certain way to avoid judgment from those around them, pretending to be what they are not. Others often admire them because they seem honest, loyal, and trustworthy. Their morality is rarely questioned when they first meet strangers, but if you spend enough time with them, cracks will begin to show in the otherwise flawless facade.

Small, nearly imperceptible slips in speech and behavior will begin to expose their true motives, and their downfall will be significant to the observant. Those initial slips will become increasingly frequent as they grow comfortable around you, and their conduct, lacking in purity and integrity, will reveal their true nature.

"But whatever comes out of the mouth proceeds from the heart, and this defiles a person. For out of the heart come evil thoughts, murder, adultery, sexual immorality, theft, false witness, and slander. These are what defiles a person...." (**Mat. 15:18-19**).

Jesus' words to His disciples serve as lessons for us as well. The warning is to guard your heart because it is the heart that reveals your authentic self-identity. In **Pro. 27:19**, we read, "As in water face reflects face, so the heart of man reflects the man." The mask worn every time they step outside is fragile – it cannot withstand the ravenous, sinful heart that is merely imprisoned when a situation calls for it. Soon, it will break free, and the individual's true identity will be unveiled. The wicked heart seeks nothing good. It acts on selfish desire, anger, and vengeance. It lacks empathy and understanding and will do whatever it takes to fulfill its own malevolent desires, regardless of the cost to the innocent.

It manifests itself in coarse language, damaging words, slanderous insults, and dangerous actions. **Jam. 4:2** states, "You desire and do not have, so you murder. You covet and cannot obtain, so you fight and quarrel." Scripture wants us to understand the dangers of an impure heart. It is selfish, self-seeking, and mean. That is why we are charged with guarding it in **Pro. 4:23**, "Keep your heart with all vigilance, for from it flow the springs of life." Of course, some people simply do not care and act in any way they want because they lack true spirituality, but we are focusing on Christians today.

We are a fallen people, and not a single individual alive today will escape stumbling from time to time. However, there is a difference between stumbling and concealing your true nature. If we truly consider ourselves servants of the Creator, that should be reflected in our conduct. James speaks about wisdom, and his words are equally valid for our heart attitude, as wisdom encompasses the scriptural knowledge that enables us to reflect who we are in Christ Jesus. "But the wisdom from above is first pure, then peaceable, gentle, open to reason, full of mercy and good fruits, impartial and sincere" (**Jam. 3:17**).

A pure heart is filled with compassion and kindness, embodying purity and love. It strives to encourage, demonstrates empathy and understanding, and prioritizes the well-being of loved ones above itself. When you pray, use the words of **Psa. 51:10**, "Create in me a pure heart, O God, and renew a steadfast spirit in me." If necessary, clean it; if you have already done so, safeguard it – it reflects who you are. Let others see that your behavior is pure and upright, and bring glory to your Father in heaven.

Chapter 53
Last, Most Desperate Thing We Do

"Rejoice always, pray without ceasing, give thanks in all circumstances; for this is the will of God in Christ Jesus for you." (**1The. 5:16**). When Nehemiah heard of a problem with the Jewish exiles and Jerusalem from Hanani, he acted without hesitation. Did he immediately ask his friends for advice or rush off to Jerusalem? No, he did not. He did not even approach the king to request leave to go to Jerusalem. In fact, it would be four months before he spoke to King Artaxerxes about the matter. Some might believe he didn't take action for a while, but what he did was not just the best possible choice under the circumstances; it also served as a lesson for all of us.

Not relying on his own wisdom for a solution, he decided to pray first. "As soon as I heard these words I sat down and wept and mourned for days, and I continued fasting and praying before the God of heaven. (**Neh. 1:4**). In **1The. 5:16**, the Greek for "ceasing," means to pray uninterruptedly and incessantly, without omission or intermission. In other words, prayer should be as automatic for a Christian as breathing is—not something we consciously think about, but rather something that happens instinctively. Prayer should be the first thing we do every morning and the last thing we do every evening, especially when faced with a challenge.

Too often, we pray for something, and when we don't receive the answer we want quickly enough, we throw our hands up in frustration. In fact, we might even feel angry with God for not listening. Sometimes, we grow weary of praying for it and simply give up, or other "more important" matters arise, and we focus on them instead. Did you know the average person thinks 12,000 to 60,000 thoughts a day? Now imagine if an eighth or even a sixteenth of those were dedicated to prayers. **Rom. 12:12** also tells us to "Be constant in prayer," and **Col. 4:2** has this to say, "Continue steadfastly in prayer."

Not convinced yet? **Php. 4:6** states, "Do not be anxious about anything, but in everything by prayer and supplication with thanksgiving let your requests be made known to God," while **Eph. 6:18** begins with, "Praying at all times in the Spirit...." Notice the common theme among the aforementioned verses? Prayer is not just one of the instruments in our spiritual toolbox; it is the primary one, and we should use it before any others. Don't worry about wearing it out—you won't. Don't fear that God will be annoyed by your constant pleas and won't answer your prayers. **Jer. 29:12** tells us that when we approach God in prayer, He hears us without exception.

Prayer clearly cannot be worn out and has no limit attached to it. Don't give up on prayer, as persistent prayer makes an impression on God and demonstrates your trust in His omnipotent timing. Failing to pray has a dangerous and unintended consequence: depending on ourselves instead of God. When we become more satisfied with physical blessings than with spiritual ones, we risk forsaking our Creator. We begin believing we can overcome any obstacle and stop relying on God for the answers. When this happens, our best-laid plans can lead us to ruin. There is nothing more ineffective in finding a solution than entering a situation unprepared. Nehemiah knew that and first asked God for direction before he acted.

Asking God for help should be the initial thing we do, not the last and most desperate one. Again, prayer should be the first thing you do in the morning and the last thing at night. Pray in the shower, while running errands, watching TV, before eating, and whenever you can spare a few moments. All the greatest characters in the Bible, including Jesus Himself, prayed unceasingly. Try it and see what happens.

Chapter 54
Fruit of the Spirit (pt. 1) Love

"But the fruit of the Spirit is love, joy, peace, patience, kindness, goodness, faithfulness, gentleness, self-control; against such things, there is no law." (**Gal. 5:22-23**). Christians possess something the world lacks. We are blessed to have been gifted with the Holy Spirit, and our lives should reflect this gift. The fruit of the Spirit consists of nine essential qualities that every Christian should embody and share so those living in darkness can see them. Now read **Mat. 5:14** with **Gal. 5:22-23** in mind;

> "You are the light of the world. A city set on a hill cannot be hidden. Nor do people light a lamp and put it under a basket, but on a stand, and it gives light to all in the house. In the same way, let your light shine before others, so that they may see your good works and give glory to your Father who is in heaven."

What light should shine before us if not the fruits of the Spirit? The world must see that we are different—not in a sad, mean, or self-serving way, but in a manner that makes them want to embrace the life we have. However, that cannot happen if we do not act in a Christ-like manner and do not display the aforementioned qualities. The first of the "fruits" may well be the one in which all the others are wrapped up. In fact, it is the primary theme of the Bible and the essence of God. Yes, the world loves too, but its love is selfish because it has man as its foundation and not the Almighty.

Even if they hate Him and their love lacks the depth and sincerity of Godly love, it still begins with God. In fact, it is impossible to love without the influence of the Almighty, whether He is accepted or rejected. **1Jo. 4:7-8**,

> "Beloved, let us love one another, for love is from God, and whoever loves has been born of God and knows God. Anyone who does not love does not know God, because God is love."

Again, without God, we would be incapable of loving. "We love because he first loved us" (**1Jo. 4:19**). You are only capable of love because God first loved you. When I think of worldly love compared to Godly love, I reflect on the following. Worldly love is self-serving; it seeks reciprocation as a reward for what is given – it is inward-focused. It embodies an "I love you because you love me" approach to affection. Conversely, Godly love is selfless and remains steadfast regardless of the recipient's feelings. I often say, "My love for you does not depend on your love for me. I don't love you because you love me; I love you because God tells me to." Godly love is outward-focused.

The command for Christians is not only to love ourselves and those close to us but all people. **1Jo. 4:21**, "And this commandment we have from him: whoever loves God must also love his brother." You cannot truly call yourself a Christian and claim to love God if you do not love your brother. In fact, we should even love our enemies. I know it sounds difficult, but it is a requirement to be called sons and daughters of the Most High God: **Mat. 5:44**, "But I say to you, Love your enemies and pray for those who persecute you, so that you may be sons of your Father who is in heaven."

We cannot leave this brief discussion on love without mentioning **Mat. 22:37-39**,

> "And he said to him, "You shall love the Lord your God with all your heart and with all your soul and with all your mind. This is the great and first commandment. And a second is like it: You shall love your neighbor as yourself."

That neighbor, by the way, refers not only to the person living next door. It encompasses everyone in the world, regardless of their ethnicity, race, religion, gender, status, power, or any other variable. Our love should be like that of the Good Samaritan and not the priest or Levite in **Luk. 10:25-37**.

Worldly love only values those who are close to the individual or those who can be exploited to advance their agenda. Godly love prioritizes the interests of others above our own and glorifies Him through our actions. If you want your light to shine before others, you must embody the fruits of the spirit and humbly showcase them to the world in a way that befits the title "Child of God." The world needs God and His love, but unless we show them what they are missing, they have nothing to strive for. Lastly, love should infuse our every thought, word, and action: **1Co. 16:14**, "Let all that you do be done in love."

Chapter 55
Fruit of the Spirit (pt. 2) Joy

"But the fruit of the Spirit is love, joy, peace, patience, kindness, goodness, faithfulness, gentleness, self-control; against such things, there is no law." (**Gal. 5:22-23**). When considering the fruit of the Spirit, joy is not merely the emotional exuberance we feel from something that brings us great happiness. That type of joy is temporary and dependent on a specific event or series of events. For instance, your favorite football team has had a great season and reached the playoffs. Throughout this journey, you experienced emotional highs when they won and crushing lows when they lost. Every playoff game they win brings you immense joy, but if they lose, all hopes for a victorious season are dashed – and sadness overwhelms you.

As you can see, joy like that results from temporary hopes being fulfilled; however, the joy Paul refers to is much more profound. Certainly, as a Christian, you will feel emotional joy, as you rightly should, but the distinction between worldly and spiritual joy becomes apparent when things do not go as expected. Peter also mentions it in **Jam. 1:2-4**,

> "Count it all joy, my brothers, when you meet trials of various kinds, for you know that the testing of your faith produces steadfastness. And let steadfastness have its full effect, that you may be perfect and complete, lacking in nothing."

The joy that both Paul and Peter refer to is not based on earthly desires but rather on heavenly hopes. The former represents "wishful thinking" and depends on others to make it happen for you. On the other hand, the latter is grounded in heaven, providing its foundation and permanence. It is not temporary or uncertain; instead, it is divine and guaranteed by the promise of God Himself. When we grasp this, we recognize that true joy is not merely an emotional state but eternal in nature, with its fulfillment found in God's aforementioned promise. The only way to experience it is to be in Christ, a son or daughter of the Creator, and to place our trust and hope in Him. And there is another significant difference. Unlike earthly joy, which leaves us exuberant only in moments of success, spiritual joy encompasses both good and bad times – it also helps us mature spiritually.

You do not truly "grow" in maturity or any noticeable way when your team wins a national or international title. For the next year, you "feel good" when talking about them, and even if they win multiple championships, eventually, that joy will be overshadowed by the disappointment of defeat. In contrast, heavenly joy serves a purpose in your life. When you know that your victory is ultimately assured and the prize exceeds anything you can imagine, your challenges will not overwhelm you. It is then that you can learn from the various trials you are bound to face. When you view them through a divine lens, they will not defeat you but allow you to grow ever closer to God as your spiritual maturity grows.

The Thessalonian church experienced that kind of joy. "And you became imitators of us and of the Lord, for you received the word in much affliction, with the joy of the Holy Spirit..." (**1 Th. 1:6**). Even amidst the challenges they encountered, the joy they derived from the Word came from the Holy Spirit, not from man. The "supernatural" joy from God is instilled in you through the Holy Spirit and becomes a source of strength when trials confront you.

Divine joy possesses the power to thwart the devil's nefarious plans, even his most meticulously crafted schemes to remove you from God's loving embrace. It accompanies not only the assurance of God's promises but also His victorious power. It is time to put aside childish, emotional joy and embrace the wonders of divine joy.

Chapter 56
Fruit of the Spirit (pt. 3) Peace

"But the fruit of the Spirit is love, joy, peace, patience, kindness, goodness, faithfulness, gentleness, self-control; against such things, there is no law." (**Gal. 5:22-23**). Peace is translated from the NT Greek word "eirene" and means "having it all together." The opposite of that could be described as chaos. When there is no peace, our lives become a mess. Without peace, there is also no order, and we remain in a constant state of unrest. A life lived like that is uncomfortable at best and, at worst, downright scary. We may also find ourselves spiritually at war, not only against the powers of darkness but also within ourselves.

Paul writes of a battle between good and evil that wages in his body in **Rom. 7:23**, "but I see in my members another law waging war against the law of my mind and making me captive to the law of sin that dwells in my members." When that happens, we find ourselves in a state of upheaval. If we fight alone, we risk growing weary and ultimately losing the battle. It is exhausting to constantly engage in a struggle—when the conflict between good and evil unfolds in our minds. Happiness eludes us, and discontentment prevails, but it doesn't have to be this way.

If peace cannot exist where chaos reigns, then the reverse is also true—when peace is present, chaos is expelled from our lives. Paul says you are to "let the peace of Christ rule in your hearts..." (**Col. 3:15**) because the sacrifice of Christ on the cross affords us that tranquility of mind, heart, and soul. The Greek meaning of the word "peace" also conveys a sense of inner tranquility and harmony. However, attaining that is not simply about feeling joyful in the face of life's challenges. That joy is fleeting, and before long, you may find yourself brought down to your knees. We cannot endure the trials of life indefinitely on our own. It requires more than that – it demands reconciliation with God to experience His power and protection. This is the source of true peace in our lives. When we direct our focus toward Christ, we can fully embrace the peace that is available to us.

It is more than simply achieving an armistice with an adversary; such a truce is fleeting because the enemy remains vigilant, constantly devising new ways to attack. The peace Paul refers to transcends that earthly understanding. It carries significance in the Hebrew word "Shalom." In ancient times, it meant restoring something to wholeness, while in later interpretations, it also came to signify "wholeness" and "well-being." When we grasp the true meaning of peace, we discover how fulfilling it can be to live by it. The absence of chaos it creates allows us to focus intently on our relationship with Christ.

No distractions lead to a clearer understanding, and a clearer understanding fosters a more obedient lifestyle. God wants you to experience peace in your life: **2Th. 3:16**, "Now may the Lord of peace himself give you peace at all times in every way. The Lord be with you all." God wants you to experience the joys of living a life free from the distractions of sin and guilt. It brings a tranquility that is beyond our understanding and provides protection as well: **Php. 4:7**, "And the peace of God, which surpasses all understanding, will guard your hearts and your minds in Christ Jesus."

A mind free of conflict is less likely to feel depressed and to experience thoughts of self-loathing or self-harm. It will not seek out the pleasures of the flesh because it fosters happiness and contentment, not sin and resentment. The pressures of life, with all its trials and tribulations, will be smoothed out, and life will be "good." And nothing—not even financial troubles, loss of health, or the passing of a loved one—can rob us of the inner tranquility it provides. Trials and loss will hurt, but the peace that surpasses all understanding will comfort and strengthen us. Try it—it is free with obedience to the scriptures.

Chapter 57
Fruit of the Spirit (pt. 4) Patience

"But the fruit of the Spirit is love, joy, peace, patience, kindness, goodness, faithfulness, gentleness, self-control; against such things, there is no law." (**Gal. 5:22-23**). The definition of patience is the "capacity to accept delay, trouble or suffering, without getting angry or upset." Many Bible versions use the word "forbearance," which essentially means the same thing. Patience is often said to be a virtue, defined as behavior reflecting a high moral standard. Therefore, patience is a trait of individuals who exhibit exemplary qualities. If we seek an example of this, we need look no further than God.

Traditionally, we refer to **2Pe. 3:9** as an example of His enduring patience, but we often overlook the 8th verse, which contextualizes it for me perfectly. The two verses read as follows,

> "But do not overlook this one fact, beloved, that with the Lord one day is as a thousand years, and a thousand years as one day. The Lord is not slow to fulfill his promise as some count slowness, but is patient toward you, not wishing that any should perish, but that all should reach repentance."

God is not constrained by time as you and I are, and His patience is perfectly characterized by its absence. Can you imagine what your future would be like if God's patience were as fickle as man's?

Many people are not long-suffering, and it doesn't take much for them to abandon those who are not toeing the line. Furthermore, I believe most of us would agree that forbearance is especially difficult during times of suffering, particularly when we can put a face and a name to the source of our pain. It is easier to wish ill on someone than to wish them well, easier to feel a strong urge for revenge than to forgive, easier to tear them down than to build them up, and easier to curse them than to pray for them.

Paul understood this when he wrote the words of **Eph. 4:1-2**,

"I therefore, a prisoner for the Lord, urge you to walk in a manner worthy of the calling to which you have been called, with all humility and gentleness, with patience, bearing with one another in love...."

Our Christian journey is filled with trials that bring difficulty and even pain, but if we want to reflect the love of God and our personal relationship with our Savior, we must cultivate this virtue. Jesus Himself exemplified long-suffering under extreme conditions: **1Pe. 2:23**, "When he was reviled, he did not revile in return; when he suffered, he did not threaten, but continued entrusting himself to him who judges justly." Vengeance is not ours, as stated in **Rom. 12:19**, so let's leave that to God and strive to remain faithful, obedient, and loving, even towards those who persecute us.

The other time we need patience is when we seek God to act on something we have prayed for—often to relieve us from the suffering we endure. Our strong desire for immediate fulfillment of our wants and needs drives us so much that we now even have "same-day delivery" from companies like Walmart and Amazon, but that is not how God operates. David was an example of patiently waiting for God to act in **Psa. 40:1-2**,

> "I waited patiently for the Lord; he inclined to me and heard my cry. He drew me up from the pit of destruction, out of the miry bog, and set my feet upon a rock, making my steps secure."

If we truly trust in God, we should also trust His timing.

You and I struggle to see beyond the present, but God is already there, looking back at us and planning to guide us to where we need to be. However, He will only do so when all the pieces are in place to make that move beneficial for us. Waiting for God to act is a sign of our confidence in His promise to restore us (**1Pe. 5:10**). What we need to be especially mindful of is trying to "go it alone" due to our impatience. This can easily lead us down the wrong path and result in even more turmoil. As children of God, we must always be patient.

Chapter 58
Fruit of the Spirit (pt. 5) Kindness

"But the fruit of the Spirit is love, joy, peace, patience, kindness, goodness, faithfulness, gentleness, self-control; against such things, there is no law." (**Gal. 5:22-23**). There is a significant lack of kindness in the world today. Being kind means being merciful, sweet, and tender, but not much of that is currently evident in society. One of the main reasons people are missing this particular fruit of the spirit is the world's complete obsession with the self. Everything must revolve around the individual. Moral absolutes like right and wrong have been replaced with moral relativism. In other words, issues like abortion, adultery, anger, envy, gender, greed, living in sin, selfish ambition, and theft are subject to the interpretation of the individual.

No one is saying that everyone must agree with everything the Bible teaches (although they should), but presently, there is no discussion about these matters—only hatred and selfish views. For a Christian, it seems unbelievable that such resistance to the ultimate moral standard can be so widespread, yet that is the reality today. We live in a world where the "I" is the only thing that matters. There is little desire for community and even less willingness to consider another's viewpoint as anything worthwhile for serious discussion. Consequently, kindness is replaced by impatience, bitterness, and even hatred.

It should not matter to a child of God how the world thinks or acts because we have a much higher authority than ourselves to follow. Therefore, we should always strive to be tenderhearted to all we encounter. The Bible tells us there is a benefit to acting this way: **Pr. 11:17**, "A man who is kind benefits himself, but a cruel man hurts himself." We are kind because God is kind. We treat others this way because our Savior expects us to, and we are kind because we love our neighbor as ourselves. God's immense kindness has led to one of His greatest gifts to humanity. **Eph. 2:4-8**,

> "But God, being rich in mercy, because of the great love with which he loved us, even when we were dead in our trespasses,

made us alive together with Christ—by grace you have been saved— and raised us up with him and seated us with him in the heavenly places in Christ Jesus so that in the coming ages he might show the immeasurable riches of his grace in kindness toward us in Christ Jesus. For by grace, you have been saved through faith. And this is not your own doing; it is the gift of God...."

If He acted out of kindness, why should we believe we should behave any differently?

The church must distinguish itself from the world – it needs to be the standard for moral integrity and kindness, demonstrating these qualities through the actions of God's family. We must also remember that being kind to someone does not imply endorsing any sinful behavior on their part. Kindness may be seen as a sign of weakness in the world, but to Christians, it represents obedience to the Word, which we regard as the final authority on earth. For those in God's household who find it difficult to embrace this spiritual fruit, the words of **Rom. 2:4** should offer encouragement to persevere: "Or do you presume on the riches of his kindness and forbearance and patience, not knowing that God's kindness is meant to lead you to repentance?"

But how can we truly repent if we show no kindness to those around us? If we do not give to others what has been given to us, we are no better than the unforgiving servant in **Mat. 18:21-35**. The mercy shown to him was not extended to another, so he was thrown into prison until he could repay his debt. God rewards us justly based on our behavior, so if we are kind to others, He will similarly be kind to us. However, if we are not... well, then He will show us none.

Chapter 59
Fruit of the Spirit (pt. 6) Goodness

"But the fruit of the Spirit is love, joy, peace, patience, kindness, goodness, faithfulness, gentleness, self-control; against such things, there is no law." (**Gal. 5:22-23**). The sixth fruit of the Spirit is "goodness," translated from the New Testament Greek word "agathosune." It signifies "uprightness of heart" and addresses not only the character trait of generosity but also how we ought to treat those we encounter. While it is easy to be good to ourselves, it is often more challenging to extend that goodness to others, especially when it requires a sacrifice on our part. Like the other fruits of the Spirit, the self-centered world often disregards the well-being of anyone aside from themselves.

Worldly people often possess an inflated sense of self-importance and entitlement, and when these traits are prevalent, generosity towards others tends to disappear. The devil deceives the unbeliever into thinking they deserve everything their hearts desire while neglecting the importance of sharing. I recall a friend who was married to a wonderful woman. When she lost her wedding ring, she was devastated. Rather than using the money they had saved to buy her a new ring, he purchased a stereo. He could have done something kind for his wife, but instead, he focused solely on his own desires.

He was blind to her anguish over losing the symbol of their wedding vows due to his desires. Worldly people like him expect and hoard whatever they can, turning a blind eye to those who are in desperate need around them. They belong to the world and follow its self-centered demands, but you do not. **Joh. 15:19** states,

> "If you were of the world, the world would love you as its own; but because you are not of the world, but I chose you out of the world, therefore the world hates you."

Since you were chosen out of this self-serving, entitled world, you must act in a Godly manner: **Gal. 6:9-10**,

"And let us not grow weary of doing good, for in due season we will reap if we do not give up. So then, as we have the opportunity, let us do good to everyone. Especially to those who are of the household of faith."

Paul suggests we should persevere in doing good because there is a reward for our ongoing efforts. It isn't solely the afterlife that Paul refers to when he mentions "in due season." While that is the ultimate reward, he also alludes to the present or near future. I recall a story I read some years ago about a young woman who worked a minimum-wage job as a cashier at a local supermarket. On several occasions, she was observed handing out some of her hard-earned money to others in need. She had no vehicle and had to wake up before sunrise to catch three different buses to reach work on time. At the end of her shift, she would repeat the process, which took three hours. Some of her regular customers were so impressed with her dedication and generosity that they purchased a vehicle for her to make her life a bit easier.

We all know stories like that, where people who did something good were rewarded in special ways. We shouldn't do it for the accolades, but it is uplifting when our efforts are recognized. There are two things we should remember when it comes to doing good. Firstly, Paul says, "...especially <to> those of the household of faith." There are too many instances of Christians neglecting to help their fellow children of God. If we cannot show non-believers that we care for each other and will be there in times of need, how can we expect them to see us as differently? Who would want to be part of a group that refuses to care for one another?

Secondly, our light shines before us when we are kind to each other and strangers **Mt. 5:16**, "In the same way, let your light shine before others so that they may see your good works and give glory to your Father who is in heaven."

Chapter 60
Fruit of the Spirit (pt. 7) Faithfulness

"But the fruit of the Spirit is love, joy, peace, patience, kindness, goodness, faithfulness, gentleness, self-control; against such things, there is no law." (**Gal. 5:22-23**). Faithfulness is essential to our Christian journey and will, more than anything else, determine our destination because it influences our obedience. In fact, the author of Hebrews clearly highlights its importance in **Heb. 11:6**, "And without faith, it is impossible to please him, for whoever would draw near to God must believe that he exists and that he rewards those who seek him."

The world has no faith in God and will have no share in the greatest promise of all time – eternal life in heaven with the Father. Instead, it places its trust in the opinions of individuals regarding the origins of humankind. The world believes in someone who identifies as a Doctor of Science, claiming to witness evidence of the universe's beginnings through a telescope. In other words, the world has faith in mankind. They lack credible evidence concerning the evolutionary development of humans, let alone the creation of the universe, yet they fall for those fanciful theories "hook, line, and sinker" nonetheless.

In the church, some people have a "kinda" faith. They "believe" in God but never attend church, pray, read their Bible, or fellowship with other Christians. They are Christians in name only, not in action, and they are as lost as those without faith in God. Neither atheists nor Christians by name only hold any hope of experiencing the unimaginable beauty of heaven. In fact, Jesus will have something to say when they attempt to plead their case to Him, but they will not be pleased to hear what He has to say: **Mat. 7:21-23**,

> "Not everyone who says to me, 'Lord, Lord,' will enter the kingdom of heaven, but the one who does the will of my Father who is in heaven. On that day many will say to me, 'Lord, Lord, did we not prophesy in your name, and cast out demons in your name, and do many mighty works in your name?' And then will I

declare to them, 'I never knew you; depart from me, you workers of lawlessness.'"

How sad that day will be for them. How unfortunate that they did not recognize their lack of faith despite their words. But it will be too late to make any changes, something I fear is lost in translation these days. Far too many believers think they will be able to bargain with Christ on the Day of Judgment, but what they don't realize is that the moments leading to their last breath on earth will be their final opportunity to change their destiny. However, there is much to be excited about for those who identify as Christians and hold on to this specific fruit of the spirit. These individuals believe in **Heb. 11:1**, "Now faith is the assurance of things hoped for, the conviction of things not seen." They rightly believe that their faithfulness determines their destiny and are entirely correct

We do not need the physical proof the world demands of us to believe in God. We see Him in everything around us: **Rom. 1:20** states, "For His invisible attributes, namely, His eternal power and divine nature, have been clearly perceived ever since the creation of the world, in the things that have been made. So, they are without excuse." We witness His majesty and glory in His creation and know He is the great "I AM." We do not believe for a second that the stars, suns, planets, earth, animals, birds, fish, insects, plants, rain, and mankind resulted from an accident.

Our faith shines because we believe, even though we have not seen, and we are incredibly joyful as we rejoice. Furthermore, we know we will be rewarded for our faithfulness. **1Pe. 1:8-9** states, "Though you have not seen him, you love him. Though you do not now see him, you believe in him and rejoice with joy that is inexpressible and filled with glory, obtaining the outcome of your faith, the salvation of your souls."

Chapter 61
Fruit of the Spirit (pt. 8) Gentleness

"But the fruit of the Spirit is love, joy, peace, patience, kindness, goodness, faithfulness, gentleness, self-control; against such things, there is no law." (**Gal. 5:22-23**). Being passionate about your religion is commendable. We should live out our Christianity and not be afraid to stand up and be counted as one of God's children. We ought to wear it as a badge of honor and not discard it whenever we are outside the church or away from our Christian circle of friends: **Rom. 1:16**, "For I am not ashamed of the gospel, for it is the power of God for salvation to everyone who believes, to the Jew first and also to the Greek."

However, some people are overly passionate, which can come off as harsh, insensitive, and angry, ultimately driving a willing ear away. If there is one thing we can be sure of, it's this: "You cannot hate anyone into the church." A lack of gentleness will push them away, and they may never return. When I was a relatively new youth minister, a teenage girl began attending church with a friend. She came from a non-churchgoing family and was unaware of the moral standards Christians adhere to, so her attire was considered "inadequate" by some adults. One well-meaning but rather harsh older woman decided to scold the teen for her clothing choices. This happened more than once. One day, it became too much for her, and she left – we never saw her at church again.

Correcting others is acceptable as long as it is done with an understanding of the person's situation and with love. We should remember Paul's words in **Tit. 3:1-2**,

> "Remind them to be submissive to rulers and authorities, to be obedient, to be ready for every good work, to speak evil of no one, to avoid quarreling, to be gentle, and to show perfect courtesy toward all people."

In the list of things Titus should remind the church to do, being gentle is mentioned, and in the very next verse, he tells them why: **Tit. 3:3**,

"For we ourselves were once foolish, disobedient, led astray, slaves to various passions and pleasures, passing our days in malice and envy, hated by others and hating one another."

We have all been there, lacking proper understanding of something at one time or another. How would it have made us feel if we were treated harshly instead of with patience and love? Our attitudes and behavior should reflect our spiritual status. Be passionate, but don't be cruel – that won't win any souls to Christ. It is for good reason that Peter encourages us to defend our spirituality with kindness: **1Pe. 3:15**, "...but in your hearts honor Christ the Lord as holy, always being prepared to make a defense to anyone who asks you for a reason for the hope that is in you; yet do it with gentleness and respect."

If we adopt the right attitude, others will respect us and be more willing to listen. However, being harsh will only create enemies and harden hearts against Christianity. In contrast, the Bible teaches us that gentleness can bring about change hearts: **2Ti. 2:24-26**, "And the Lord's servant must not be quarrelsome but kind to everyone, able to teach, patiently enduring evil, correcting his opponents with gentleness. God may perhaps grant them repentance leading to a knowledge of the truth, and they may come to their senses and escape from the devil's snare after being captured by him to do his will."

This eighth fruit of the Spirit should also be fully evident to those in the household of God who are struggling: **Gal. 6:1**, "Brothers, if anyone is caught in any transgression, you who are spiritual should restore him in a spirit of gentleness...." Finally, I think the words of **Mat. 7:12** gives us an excellent reason why we should be gentle, "So whatever you wish that others would do to you, do also to them....

Chapter 62
Fruit of the Spirit (pt. 9) Self-control

"But the fruit of the Spirit is love, joy, peace, patience, kindness, goodness, faithfulness, gentleness, self-control; against such things, there is no law." (**Gal. 5:22-23**). If there is one thing a Christian needs in abundance, it is self-control. When we have it, we can manage our emotions and behavior. Self-control helps us avoid conforming to the world and enables us to say "no" to sin. Paul tells us in **Rom. 12:2** to resist the pressure to conform to the world and instead be transformed: "Do not be conformed to this world, but be transformed by the renewal of your mind, that by testing you may discern what is the will of God, what is good and acceptable and perfect."

The world often lacks self-control due to its reactive nature. It assumes that the best form of defense is attack and fails to take a moment to seriously consider the consequences. When something happens to a non-Christian, extreme anger frequently becomes the immediate response, leading to a downward spiral from that moment on. Another consequence of the absence of this particular fruit of the Spirit is the ease with which individuals succumb to sin. There is no defense against drugs, pornography, adultery, alcohol, and various other sins that can invade the life of someone lacking self-control.

Even in the church, a lack of discipline can lead individuals down a dangerous path, preventing them from resisting sin. When this occurs, sins like gossip and pride can flourish, allowing discord to grow into unhappiness and disunity. Thoughtless words can be spoken, leading to friendships dissolving into contempt and even hatred. The writer of **Pro. 25** compares a person without self-control to a city without walls. Without adequate barriers, the enemy can launch an unimpeded attack from any direction and overthrow that city: **Pro. 25:28**, "A man without self-control is like a city broken into and left without walls." To lack self-discipline is to dishonor God and to make a mockery of Him in the eyes of the world.

When the worldly person sees a Christian easily consenting to sin, they judge all of Christianity by that standard, and it may harden a receptive heart as a result. Various behaviors require discipline, including overeating, overspending, overindulging, and overreacting. For most people, the temptation to indulge in the appealing things of the world often outweighs the fear of consequences, especially when those consequences are far off. Imagine if a child could consume as much candy as they wished. Naturally, they would overindulge because they lack the discipline and understanding of the long-term effects of their actions. The same can be said for some Christians.

We have a dangerous tendency to throw discipline out the window and fail to consider the long-term consequences of our actions. We may believe that sin leads to death, but we do not recognize how imminent that death might be, so we continue on as if we are oblivious to the associated dangers. Paul conveys this message to Timothy in **2Ti. 1:7**, "...for God gave us a spirit not of fear but of power and love and self-control." When we have the Holy Spirit, we possess a spiritual strength that empowers us to overcome our weak, fallen human nature, allowing us to resist the temptations of sin.

In the end, there is a battle within our minds. On one side, we have the devil and his temptations designed to pull us away from God's loving embrace; on the other side, we have God and the Spirit of power, love, and self-control. If we are victorious, we will have the strength to set aside the things of this world and pursue what is more glorious and heavenly. We will find it easier to experience all the fruits of the Spirit when we cultivate and maintain self-discipline.

It will also help us compare the fleeting nature of sin to the unimaginable beauty of God's kingdom. Perhaps we could memorize and recite the words of **Psa. 84:10** when we falter with our discipline, "For a day in your courts is better than a thousand elsewhere. I would rather be a doorkeeper in the house of my God than dwell in the tents of wickedness."

Chapter 63
Preach the Word of God, not Man

"Preach the word; be ready in season and out of season; reprove, rebuke, and exhort, with complete patience and teaching" (**2Ti. 4:2**). In his final charge to his understudy, Paul aims to impress upon Timothy the urgency of continuing his work. Since the context involves one evangelist guiding another, we will first examine that relationship and then address the broader audience. Not everyone is called to preach; it is a daunting task that can be psychologically challenging. When Paul states, "preach the word," he underscores the importance of perseverance despite hardships, and one thing any new minister can be assured of is that difficult times are both expected and plentiful.

How can you know if you should be a preacher? Let's refer to Paul's words in **1Co. 9:16** for clarity on that question: "For if I preach the gospel, that gives me no ground for boasting. For necessity is laid upon me. Woe to me if I do not preach the gospel!" The second sentence says it all. Preaching is not something you do because someone thinks you will be good at it. It is not something you pursue because you woke up one morning, read a verse or two, and thought, "Hmm, this could be enjoyable." It is also not something you should undertake if you believe you are all-knowing. There is no room for arrogance in

Preaching is a calling so strong that nothing can prevent you from doing it— not even yourself. It is for you if you cannot imagine yourself doing anything else. If that is your choice, preaching must be biblical, not personal. "Preaching the word" does not involve your ideas or even what you have been taught in a Bible college or university. It is God's "oracles" (revelation) and not the endless thoughts committed to ink by some scholars. Certainly, educated individuals who have taken the time to exegete scripture thoughtfully will always be valuable tools for a preacher, but they should not be the primary source. Far too many "men of God" rely on human works for their material and then use God's word to support it instead of vice versa.

That is a recipe for disaster because it allows the agenda of manmade materials to cloud your exegesis. Paul did not instruct Timothy to read endless books authored by humans but instead to focus on the material available to him that was inspired by God. This idea is reflected in the words of **2Ti 3:16-17**,

> "All Scripture is breathed out by God and profitable for teaching, for reproof, for correction, and for training in righteousness, that the man of God may be complete, equipped for every good work."

Speaking the oracles of God can be uncomfortable at times. It often contradicts the wishes of the masses and sometimes even our own, but we are not speaking for ourselves when we preach; we are speaking for God – and that can lead to trouble. Even those closest to you may disagree and despise you for it.

Substantive preaching is devoid of analogy after analogy, endless stories, illustrations, and so on; instead, it is exegetical in nature. In other words, the meaning is derived from the passage, not from humans. Herein lies the danger of consulting books before the Bible, as this approach can lead to what is known as eisegesis (reading meaning into a verse). Now, what about those who are not specifically preachers? What should they do? It's actually simple: they should follow the same practice.

While only a few are called to careers in pulpit preaching, we are all called to make disciples (**Mat. 28:18-20**). Thus, we all engage in preaching and teaching to some extent. So, when Paul says, "preach the word," it applies to everyone desiring to honor God's word. Study the Bible before considering human writings, and preach the word rather than man's thoughts and agenda.

Chapter 64
Be Careful of a Large Hammer

"Preach the Word; be ready in season and out of season; reprove, rebuke, and exhort, with complete patience and teaching" (**2Ti. 4:2**). After Timothy is charged to preach the Word, he is told by his mentor, Paul, always to be ready. That admonishment applies to us as well. We must always be prepared to preach the Gospel to those seeking the truth. To do this effectively, we must study the Bible diligently; however, I fear that this is a somewhat forgotten practice for most people. Not only should we be ready to preach the Good News, but we should also teach with complete patience, not allowing our frustration over their slight resistance to affect us.

Sharing the Gospel is not only for certain people like the preacher or the elders; each of us has a command from Jesus to evangelize all the time: **Mat. 28:18-20,**

> "And Jesus came and said to them, "All authority in heaven and on earth has been given to me. Go therefore and make disciples of all nations, baptizing them in the name of the Father and of the Son and of the Holy Spirit, teaching them to observe all that I have commanded you. And behold, I am with you always, to the end of the age."

Timothy, and by extension, all of us, do not have forever to convince the unbeliever of their need for salvation. There will never be a convenient time because the next moment is not guaranteed to anyone.

Now, that doesn't mean we have to be "Bible-punchers" and forcefully declare the Word to those who are not willing to hear it. People who subscribe to this type of pushiness often refer to the words of Jesus in the Parable of the Great Banquet. When the invited guests made excuses for not attending the feast, the owner told his servants in **Luk. 14:23**, "Go out to the highways and hedges and compel people to come in, that my house may be filled." They argue that Jesus advocates forcing the lost to listen and be saved. Their mistake lies not in the concept but in its execution. It is not through physical force or demanding attention to our message that we will compel them, but through convincing arguments that cannot be ignored. This is clearly illustrated by the three words: "reprove, rebuke, and exhort."

We can use modern equivalents to better understand the urgency these words convey. "Convince, reprimand, and encourage" urges the possibly somewhat hesitant Timothy to be more proactive in sharing the Word. Some individuals we meet are more receptive when we strongly persuade them with facts. Others might engage us in spirited debates. A third group may not respond well to either of the first two approaches or even a combination of them. They might be more open to a message of love and hope or an invitation to casually attend a service. Either way, it would be beneficial for anyone initiating a discussion with a nonbeliever to discern the temperament and personality of the person they are speaking with.

Applying pressure this way will ensure that it is appropriate and does not lead to negative consequences. If we are too forceful and try to force the Word upon someone receptive but not fully ready to commit, we risk turning an open heart into a hardened one. Using a large hammer to drive in a small nail may cause irreparable damage to the nail. Sometimes, it's much more effective to gently tap the nail, taking as much time as needed to drive it in successfully.

The best way to approach the unbeliever with the Gospel is detailed at the end of the verse: "with complete patience and teaching." Never let your enthusiasm to bring them to the waters of baptism overshadow your patience in dealing with them gently. As the saying goes, "Rome was not built in a day."

There's a caution that authorities often use against speeding that I like to apply in this context: "Speed kills." Moving too quickly may lead to results that are opposite to what we are praying for. Instead of leading to salvation, we could extinguish their spiritual life. Sometimes, it is better to plant the seed, allow someone else to nurture it, and then let God provide the growth in His time. **1Cor. 3:6**, "I planted, Apollos watered, but God gave the growth."

Chapter 65
Instant Gratification = Eternal Regret

"There are some things in them (scriptures) that are hard to understand, which the ignorant and unstable twist to their own destruction, as they do the other Scriptures" (**2Pe. 3:16**). In his final words to the church, Peter urges them to hold fast to their hope in God and offers one last warning. These words serve as a warning for us as well. Today's greatest danger is not political division, racial baiting, class warfare, or economic instability. It is not even the ever-present threat of another global war or a dangerous pandemic breaking out. While any of these threats can be devastating, none are as inherently dangerous or carry the long-term destructive consequences of twisting the scriptures.

You see, "to their own destruction" does not refer to temporary discomfort, pain, or even death, but rather to an eternity in the fiery lake of hell. Again, I do not want you to think that I am making light of the dangers I mentioned earlier, which can cause us tremendous heartache and grief; we all know they can. People's lives could be turned upside down by them, and they could lose all their material possessions and possibly be psychologically traumatized. However, while we all sympathize deeply with those undergoing such trials, we must be aware of the dangers of twisting the scriptures.

In fact, there is a stark warning against that practice in the book of Revelation: **Rev. 22:18-19,**

> "I warn everyone who hears the words of the prophecy of this book: if anyone adds to them, God will add to him the plagues described in this book, and if anyone takes away from the words of the book of this prophecy, God will take away his share in the tree of life and in the holy city, which are described in this book."

One might think those words would serve as a strong enough warning to deter anyone from intentionally misinterpreting the scriptures, but unfortunately, that is not the reality. Millions of people gladly alter the scriptures to fit their own agendas or emotional needs. The Bible does not grant them the freedom to act as they wish or live according to their desires; thus, they modify it.

Some even go so far as to leave out parts entirely to indulge their lustful passions. Even when sin is not the goal, misinterpreting God's Holy Word for personal gain will lead to severe consequences of a scale we cannot begin to comprehend. We should read the Bible with the intent of fulfilling the will of God rather than our emotions. Neither the Bible nor the church exists for our pleasure, and none of it "comes from someone's own interpretation" (**2Pe. 1:20**) or was "ever produced by the will of man…" (**2Pe. 2:21**). We did not create man; God did. We did not write the Bible; God did. It is not our words but His.

In the epistle to Timothy, Paul reminds us that "All Scripture is breathed out by God and profitable for teaching, for reproof, for correction, and for training in righteousness" (**2Ti. 3:16**). We do not have the right to change what is not ours to change. We are mortal, and our lives are fleeting. What right do we have to alter that which is eternal? **Jam. 1:17** states, "Every good gift and every perfect gift is from above, coming down from the Father of lights, with whom there is no variation or shadow due to change." His Word is one of the most precious gifts we have, and we should honor it by never misrepresenting its contents. We are born with a strong desire to make our lives more comfortable according to our personal needs, but we should resist that desire when it means tampering with God's Holy Word. Don't be one of those individuals who change what seems difficult into something "more bearable." Always remember this: "Instant gratification = eternal regret."

Chapter 66
Which One Are You?

"Hear then the Parable of the sower: When anyone hears the word of the kingdom and does not understand it, the evil one comes and snatches away what has been sown in his heart. This is what was sown along the path. As for what was sown on rocky ground, this is the one who hears the word and immediately receives it with joy, yet he has no root in himself, but endures for a while, and when tribulation or persecution arises on account of the word, immediately he falls away.

As for what was sown among thorns, this is the one who hears the word, but the cares of the world and the deceitfulness of riches choke the word, and it proves unfruitful. As for what was sown on good soil, this is the one who hears the word and understands it. He indeed bears fruit and yields, in one case a hundredfold, in another sixty, and in another thirty."

(**Mat. 13:18-23**).

These verses explain **Mat. 13:3-9**, but for the sake of brevity, I did not include them. Feel free to read them if you are not already familiar with the Parable. Many seeds are sown on the path. They listen to what is said, but it all seems confusing and complicated, leaving them spiritually weak. They take the message to heart but do not hold onto it tightly. The evil one then comes along and, with little effort, snatches away what they have heard. However, this can also happen if we overwhelm them with more information than they can absorb or push too forcefully

Even while you're speaking to them, their minds are devising a plan to escape the torment of your Bible-thumping. They are easy targets, and Satan doesn't have to work too hard to pull them back into his fold. The second type of seed, thrown on rocky ground, represents all the "eager-beavers" who rush into baptism without fully understanding what it entails. They don't study afterward, read their Bible, pray, or attend church regularly. They are "good-time," emotionally driven "Christians" who stumble at the first sign of trouble and then abandon the constraints of godly living. Those individuals half-heartedly don the armor of God but don't actually secure it or pick up any weapons.

When the assault from the evil one comes, they quickly throw up their hands in defeat and are dragged into captivity once again. Then we have the "sown among the thorns" seeds, which "kind of" gladly accept the Gospel message but never truly commit to it. We have all encountered someone like this – the person who thinks about committing and talks about committing but finds the things of the world too alluring, so they leave. These individuals will never let something as silly as forgiveness or "turn from your sins" interfere with having a good time.

Now, if Christianity could just ease up a bit and be more understanding of its followers' desires, they would be all-in. And that "love your neighbor" thing isn't going to happen...ever. They will not give up their vices and selfish ambitions to follow some religious mumbo-jumbo. Of course, some listen intently, process and understand the message, hold it tightly and close to their hearts, and don the armor of God, ready to successfully repel the devil's attacks. They don't just study until baptism either – they become lifelong students of the Word and grow in maturity and dedication daily. They make a difference for the Lord's Kingdom and will receive their reward—the crown of life. Let me ask you something today: which one are you?

Chapter 67

The Power of His Whisper

"...Go out and stand on the mount before the Lord." And behold, the Lord passed by, and a great and strong wind tore the mountains and broke the rocks before the Lord, but the Lord was not in the wind. And after the wind an earthquake, but the Lord was not in the earthquake. And after the earthquake, a fire, but the Lord was not in the fire. And after the fire, the sound of a low whisper. And when Elijah heard it, he wrapped his face in his cloak and went out and stood at the cave entrance. And behold, there came a voice to him and said, "What are you doing here, Elijah?" (**1Ki. 19:11-13**).

After Elijah killed hundreds of false Baal prophets, he was afraid Queen Jezebel would have him killed, so he fled to Horeb, the mount of God, and found a cave there. He was instructed to stand on the mountain before the Lord during his time in that cave. Elijah must have felt quite scared at that point in his life. Fear is not always negative; it often protects you from making foolish choices that could lead to significant harm. If you stand on the edge of a 100-foot cliff overlooking the ocean, I bet you will think twice before jumping. In fact, I am certain that 99.99% of people would be far too scared to jump – and that is a good thing.

We don't walk around in the middle of the night in dangerous areas of a city because we are afraid of being mugged—which is also a good thing. Fear can keep us safe. The old adage, "Better safe than sorry," should always guide your thoughts. Was Elijah unnecessarily scared? Maybe, but he wasn't willing to take any chances. Of course, one could argue that God granted him a magnificent victory, so he shouldn't have been afraid. However, keep in mind that even heroes can experience fear, so perhaps we should cut the prophet some slack, so to speak. So why did God send the wind, the earthquake, and the fire?

Some say Elijah wanted God to destroy his enemies with one or more devastating natural disasters. Others argue that Elijah felt discouraged because, although he had triumphed over the prophets of Baal, he believed he had failed to lead the people back to God. Regardless, God's purpose was to demonstrate that His true power lies in His word, not in dramatic, natural, or even miraculous events. In **Jer. 23:29**, we read, "Is not My word like fire, declares the Lord, and like a hammer that breaks the rock in pieces?" Earlier, Elijah defeated all those false prophets but thought he had not been successful, despite the reality of the "7,000" who renewed their faith in verse 18.

Clearly, God controls all the forces of nature and can use them to His advantage, but that is not His preferred way of operating. I believe millions of Christians wait to hear God act in the strong winds, shake the earth with an earthquake, or burn everything to the ground. That is how they expect God to act, and when He does not, they feel confused and become discouraged. When they don't see them, they falter or turn to the world for solutions, but that only weakens their Christian resolve, and before long, they have left Christ far behind in the rearview mirror of sin.

They are like the Pharisees in **Mat. 16:1-4**,

> "And the Pharisees and Sadducees came, and to test him they asked him to show them a sign from heaven. He answered them, "When it is evening, you say, 'It will be fair weather, for the sky is red.' And in the morning, 'It will be stormy today, for the sky is red and threatening.' You know how to interpret the appearance of the sky, but you cannot interpret the signs of the times. An evil and adulterous generation seeks a sign, but no sign will be given to it except the sign of Jonah." So he left them and departed."

Don't be like them. They didn't receive explosive signs, and you probably won't, either. Instead of waiting for visible manifestations of His power, why not go to a place where you can leave the world's noise behind and focus on hearing His whisper? God doesn't have to prove He is God – He is God, period. He works all things to His delight in a gentle, concentrated, focused, and meaningful way. The power of His whisper is all you need.

Chapter 68
Religious Freedom?

"But understand this, that in the last days there will come times of difficulty. For people will be lovers of self, lovers of money, proud, arrogant, abusive, disobedient to their parents, ungrateful, unholy, heartless, unappeasable, slanderous, without self-control, brutal, not loving good, treacherous, reckless, swollen with conceit, lovers of pleasure rather than lovers of God" (**2Ti. 3:1-8**).

I know those words don't only apply to the present, but it certainly feels as if Paul had a crystal ball and peered into the world of 2022-23 when he wrote them. Many countries have Christians who are persecuted daily for their beliefs. If they are lucky, slander is all they endure, but if they are not, beatings and even death could be in their future.

We look at those countries and consider ourselves fortunate to live in the "Good ole USA," where religious freedom is a constitutional right. Not having to worry about our ability to assemble safely as we praise our God and Father is a blessing we should never take for granted. This morning, we will examine this religiously free country more closely. Now, I don't want to be a "Debbie-downer," but the direction we began moving in from around the '60s should be concerning, if not quite alarming. In 1962, the first case against prayer in schools was won with the Snyder versus Vitale case.

In 1963, the famous Madaline O'Hare (Murray versus Curlett) succeeded in removing prayer from all schools. Ironically, her son, William O'Hare, would later become a preacher and a strong advocate for reintroducing prayer in schools. In 1968, the ban on teaching evolution in schools was ruled unconstitutional, while the prohibition of creationism has never received the same distinction. In 1980, the Supreme Court decided that displaying the Ten Commandments in a school classroom violated the Constitution. Additionally, in 1985, the Supreme Court ruled that a moment of silence in schools is unconstitutional if it is intended to promote prayer. Around that time, all nativity scenes in government buildings were also declared unconstitutional.

In 1992, the Supreme Court ruled that allowing a clergy member to recite a prayer in elementary and secondary schools was unconstitutional. In 2001, a federal district court decided that a teacher should be removed from a classroom because the instructor was a creationist and, therefore, could not adequately teach evolution. There are many other cases in which the Supreme Court, District Court, or other government entities effectively challenged Christianity, but I want to focus on the examples involving schools for a specific reason. A few years ago, I was told that Apple decided to offer great deals on their computers to as many universities as possible.

That strategy was sheer brilliance. If they placed their computers in the hands of college students, they would be more likely to continue using them both privately and in the workplace after graduation. This parallels the approach of the Separation of Religion and State organization, the Supreme Court, and many other anti-Christian organizations in our country. They advocate openly and loudly for the removal of all Christian references from schools. In doing so, they effectively diminish the Bible's significance in young students' minds. Furthermore, this nearly eliminates any chance of introducing young children to the gospel in school.

Although technically the opposite of the Apple strategy, this approach is equally effective. We thank God every day for living in a country where we enjoy religious freedom, but we must remain aware that the church is under attack daily. We should pray fervently that our freedom to practice our religion endures.

Chapter 69
What Do You Think Your Soul Is Worth?

> "And He said to all, "If anyone would come after Me, let him deny himself and take up his cross daily and follow Me. For whoever would save his life will lose it, but whoever loses his life for My sake will save it. For what does it profit a man if he gains the whole world and loses or forfeits himself?" (**Luk. 9:23-25**).

Jesus conveys much in these three verses. Firstly, He instructs us to deny ourselves. While many interpret this as a rejection of our sinful nature, and I partially agree, I argue that it is more about denying ourselves as the main focus in favor of Christ. As long as we prioritize ourselves, Jesus will never be the central object of our desires and obedience.

When that is the case, our obedience will be to ourselves first. In other words, we will continue to be the self-centered, selfish sinners we are born as. Next, Jesus tells us to take up our cross and follow Him daily. Since a criminal accused of rebelling against authority was often forced to carry his own cross to the site of his crucifixion, Jesus' words hold a compelling meaning for us. The purpose of carrying one's cross to the place of execution was a sign of the complete defeat of their rebellion. Similarly, carrying our cross symbolizes the total defeat of our spiritual rebellion.

Doing this daily signifies surrender to God's power, grace, and mercy through His Son, Jesus Christ. It also reflects our humble obedience to His absolute authority in our lives. The last thing Jesus mentions is the cost of our souls. What occurs when we attempt to save our lives by conforming to the ways of the world? Jesus clearly states that we will lose it, not physically at this moment, but more terrifyingly, on the Day of Judgment. The issue is that most people seem unafraid of the repercussions of choosing to save their own lives outside of Christianity. They accumulate the things of the world—the glittering, shiny treasures that appeal to the flesh—and store them away to boast about, indulge in, and display as signs of wealth and status.

Mat. 6:19-20, "Do not lay up for yourselves treasures on earth, where moth and rust destroy and where thieves break in and steal, but lay up for yourselves treasures in heaven, where neither moth nor rust destroys and where thieves do not break in and steal."

Can you imagine the cries of anguish and torment on that Day when Jesus looks at them and declares, "I never knew you; depart from Me...." What benefit will all the world's wealth, status, and adoration be then? Absolutely nothing- those things will not be the bargaining chips some may think they are. Let me ask you something today: What do you think your soul is worth? What would you pay for it? A thousand dollars? A million? Fame or fortune? Family and friends? Money and the security it brings.

Unfortunately, the price is too high for most people in the world. They are simply unwilling to sacrifice the luxuries or accolades of life to receive the crown of life promised to those who embrace Christ and remain obedient. Even if they feel mildly threatened by Jesus' words, they think they have time. They believe the Day of Judgment is too far in the future to take seriously right now. They either don't care or think tomorrow will bring another chance, so they persist in the misguided delusion of their desires to satisfy their need for immediate gratification.

They do not know their expiration date, so they live as if it will happen far in the future. Sadly, most will meet their doom because of this false belief. Life's fleeting pleasures are simply not worth sacrificing your salvation for. Everyone must heed the warning that our end could come at any moment and be prepared to pay any price necessary to receive the reward of an eternity in heaven. Those who deny themselves, take up their cross, and lose their lives will have a completely different ending to their stories than those who attempt to save them. They will receive the Crown of Life and be welcomed into heaven.

Chapter 70
He Is Waiting to Hear from You

"In my distress, I called upon the Lord; to my God, I cried for help. From His temple He heard my voice, and my cry to Him reached his ears" (**Psa. 18:6**). Have you ever found yourself in a dire situation where you felt psychologically and physically brutalized by something or someone? What did you do? Did you try to flee or stay and fight? In situations ranging from mild discomfort to life-threatening danger, we generally have those two options. Sure, there are others, but we will focus on these two for this article because any other response would stem from one of those two. Every other response, that is, except one.

Many people forget that before the fight or flight response, there is a crucial step that should always be the first one taken. When we exclude this step, we are left to our own devices, and very often, the decisions we make as a result lack the guidance of the Almighty. We are then left with these two extreme options. While both are valid under certain conditions, they should only occur after that first, all-important step. King David understood this and called out to God in his moments of distress.

Heaven, the dwelling place of God, seems far away. How can God hear us from such a great distance—one that surpasses human limits? A distance so immense that we cannot travel from one side to the other and back again. Although God dwells in heaven, His omnipresence means He is truly everywhere, and why wouldn't He be, considering all of this is His creation? Do you wish to know how close He is? Let's read the words of **Act. 17:25-28**,

> "...nor is He served by human hands, as though He needed anything, since He himself gives to all mankind life and breath and everything. And He made from one man every nation of mankind to live on all the face of the earth, having determined allotted periods and the boundaries of their dwelling place, that they should seek God, and perhaps feel their way toward Him and

find Him. Yet He is actually not far from each one of us, for" 'In Him we live and move and have our being'; as even some of your own poets have said," 'For we are indeed His offspring.'"

How do we live in Him, you may ask? Well, another scripture will answer that question for us. **1Co. 6:19** states, "Or do you not know that your body is a temple of the Holy Spirit within you, whom you have from God?" That's right; the Holy Spirit dwells in you, but when does He begin His stay with you, you may now wonder? Once again, let's turn to God's word for the answer. **Act. 2:38** says,

"And Peter said to them, "Repent and be baptized every one of you in the name of Jesus Christ for the forgiveness of your sins, and you will receive the gift of the Holy Spirit.'"

You don't need to scream or shout for God to hear you. You don't have to send Him an email or a letter through the postal service. In fact, you don't even need to speak out loud or in a whisper. You can simply think the words in your mind, and God will hear you. And just like David, He listens when you call out to God. Will He respond? If you are His child, absolutely. **Joh. 9:31** states, "We know that God does not listen to sinners, but if anyone is a worshiper of God and does His will, God listens to him." Don't let the perceived distance intimidate you; it isn't as great as you think. Don't be afraid; God wants to hear from you and won't penalize you for interrupting His busy day. In fact, He will bless you for doing so

Will He answer the way you want? Maybe, or maybe not, but you will get an answer. Call on Him and then trust Him to know the best solution, remaining faithful whether you understand it or not. Remember, God is always waiting to hear from you and to respond to you in a way that is best for you.

Chapter 71
Who Is Your Focus?

"Jesus said to him, 'I am the way, and the truth, and the life. No one comes to the Father except through Me" (**Joh. 14:6**). There is a significant problem in many churches today. It affects some Christians and even certain congregations, and it has the potential to close the doors of churches across the country and, indeed, the world. This issue arises from a fundamental lack of loyalty. When Jesus declares that He is the way, the truth, and the life, and that there is no other path to heaven, He is, by definition, excluding any mortal. No minister can provide what Jesus can. Ministers should live and preach the Word effectively, equipping listeners with knowledge and the desire to embrace Christ in baptism and remain faithful.

Sermons should be exegetical in nature, encouraging and instructing the listener. They should also serve as a source of comfort, a recognition of their current state, a strengthening of their spiritual armor against the evil one's attacks, and, at times, a serious admonition regarding sin in their lives. However, one aspect should never overshadow any of this: the focus should never be on them, and the message should never be about them.

In many churches, leadership is followed in an almost cult-like manner. No matter what the leader does, the faithful will adore and follow blindly—much like the children who followed the Pied Piper in that famous story. They disregard **Tit. 2:1**, "But as for you, teach what accords with sound doctrine," while the ministers carefully craft their messages. They teach from the heart instead of from the Word, preach to emotions rather than to the intellect, and rely on productions and stories rather than the Gospel. Additionally, the messages tend to be politically correct rather than doctrinally sound. Even well-meaning preachers can fall into the trap of trying to avoid offending anyone for fear of offending someone and losing a congregant.

Here is the point I want to make this morning. If you attend a particular church because you have the "best preacher in the world," there is nothing wrong with that—as long as he adheres to scripture and is not the primary reason for your attendance. There is nothing wrong with appreciating a man of God who delivers powerful, accurate, and encouraging messages. Still, you should reconsider your situation and current location if you are drawn solely to him instead of the Word. When he becomes "He," when he becomes the focus of your life; when what he says takes precedence over any message from the Bible; when he is the final authority in your life; when he is the "reason," you need to fervently pray to be freed from that delusional, indoctrinated devotion. God before man always!

It is not for nothing that the words of **Act. 4:12** is written in God's inspired Word: "And there is salvation in no one else, for there is no other name under heaven given among men by which we must be saved." When you find yourself more in love with the preacher than with Jesus, you are in a precarious situation with a horrific forever attached to it. Don't go to church just to see and hear him. He is merely one of many vehicles that can move you closer to God through exegetical preaching. Your commitment to a specific church should be based on the soundness of the teachings and the fellowship you experience there.

Love him only as a sound preacher, dedicated husband, father, dear friend, and committed leader who exemplifies his teachings. Who is your focus?

Chapter 72
Don't Squander God's Gifts

> "For as in one body we have many members, and the members do not all have the same function, so we, though many, are one body in Christ, and individually members one of another. Having gifts that differ according to the grace given to us, let us use them: if prophecy, in proportion to our faith; if service, in our serving; the one who teaches, in his teaching; the one who exhorts, in his exhortation; the one who contributes, in generosity; the one who leads, with zeal; the one who does acts of mercy, with cheerfulness" (**Rom. 12:4-8**).

As I read these verses, I often reflect on our gifts and how we utilize them, if we do at all. One of the joys of gathering as a community in a place we like to call church is that we can combine our diverse gifts for the betterment of the church to the glory of God. None of us can do everything well. We may think we are Jack-of-all-trades, but we are likely weaker in some areas than others. The key is to recognize that the true power of the church lies in teamwork. Not everyone can be a preacher. Not everyone can be a teacher or a disciple-maker, but we are all at least good at one thing. All we need to do is pray about it, discover it, and then use it for the greater good of God's Kingdom.

Let's say that teaching is your passion. You possess enormous patience and eagerly research any given topic. You dedicate multiple hours to preparing an effective, biblically sound lesson to instruct, empower, and encourage your class. You recognize the significance of learning. Perhaps you are a door greeter—someone with a beautiful smile, a kind word of welcome, and a warm, inviting handshake or hug. You represent a visitor's first impression of the church and wouldn't have it any other way. You set the tone for the morning or evening with your loving, personable attitude. You realize the importance of making people feel welcome right from the start.

Perhaps you are a disciple-maker. You enjoy spontaneous encounters with strangers and never miss the chance to invite them to discover Christ. You aren't afraid to share the gospel with anyone you meet, and people listen to you because you have a knack for making friends. You recognize the importance of ministering to those still lost in sin. Perhaps you are getting older, and teaching or standing at the door isn't for you anymore. Instead of those responsibilities, you find joy in calling and sending cards to guests and those who couldn't attend the service. You are the person who picks up the phone and says, "Hey, we missed you at church this morning. I just wanted to check in and let you know we love you."

You love selecting unique cards for special occasions and surprising the fortunate recipients on their special days. You recognize the importance of staying in touch. Perhaps you can't do that anymore due to personal challenges, and that's okay because you find joy in praying. You can spend hours doing so, naming person after person as you petition God on their behalf. You understand the power of prayer. Maybe you excel in technology and want to manage the website or social media accounts. Perhaps you enjoy organizing upcoming events and meals, are well-suited for cleaning the building or maintaining the yard, or enjoy visiting the sick and infirmed.

Regardless of which gifts you have, whether mentioned above or others, it's important to use them for God's glory. The leadership of your church should meet with you and encourage you to identify your gifts and utilize them as well. If you feel you are not being utilized to your fullest potential, consider if God is calling you to make a change – to seek a place that values your passion for making a difference and will engage you where you will be most effective.

Chapter 73
The Dangers of Being Unequally Yoked

"My son, fear the Lord and the king, and do not join with those who do otherwise" (**Pro. 24:21**). A Christian teenager once asked me if he could befriend an unbeliever. He really liked this kid at his school but struggled with his behavior. Around that time, a girl in the youth group was very clear about the behavior she expected from her friends. If they used foul language or made crude jokes, she would reprimand them and make it known that she preferred not to be friends with them if they continued.

I began to ask my Christian friends and fellow ministers what views they held, and the responses I received were as varied as the types of people I asked. One parent told me, "Absolutely not. I will not see my daughter dragged into jail because of some little heathen." He even had a quote from Proverbs on hand, as if he had been asked this question before." **1Co. 15:33**, "Do not be deceived: Bad company ruins good morals." I asked him if his children were homeschooled, and he replied, "No!" I could not help but wonder how that was working out for him. When we surround our children with the world, and there is almost no way we can totally prevent that from happening, we expect them to be close to some unbelievers, don't we?

Another parent shared that she trusted her daughter's ability to discern between good and bad friends, so she felt comfortable with her child's choices. When I asked her if she had a verse to support her position, she happily recited one of my favorites. **Pro. 27:17**, "Iron sharpens iron, and one man sharpens another." She argued that her daughter would positively influence the other child, potentially leading that person to seek a relationship with Christ. "Do you monitor her friendships?" I inquired. "I am not the "friends police.' I trust her, and that's all there is to it," she replied. Her complete trust was almost commendable if it weren't for the apparent dangers her daughter could encounter.

A third parent mentioned she didn't mind but carefully monitored the friendship to ensure things didn't go south. She expressed her view: "I believe it's important for her to be exposed to everyone, but I must make sure she stays on the narrow road. I also try to ensure she makes informed choices regarding friends." Is she the wisest of the three parents? The Bible allows friendship with the world, but it clearly warns us of the dangers in verses like **2Co. 6:14**, which states, "Do not be unequally yoked with unbelievers. For what partnership has righteousness with lawlessness? Or what fellowship has light with darkness?" If both parties don't have equal footing in the relationship, the Christian should distance themselves from it before their morals are compromised

If my wife hadn't agreed to be my girlfriend, I wouldn't have found Christ and wouldn't be a minister today. I never prevented my children from being friends with unbelievers, and more than one of them became baptized believers as a result. However, I would caution parents to be careful. We know how impressionable kids can be, and they can easily be drawn away from God's loving hands by their peers. Yet, we are not excluded from that danger ourselves.

We may not be as impressionable, but we can still be drawn into a dangerous relationship. We must be equally cautious in making wise choices about the type of friends we select, and we should recognize when it's time to end a friendship if necessary. Friendships allow us to invite people to share in the "...assurance of things hoped for..." (**Heb. 11:1**), but we need to be mindful of the risks of being unequally yoked.

Chapter 74
Pay no Attention to Them

"But concerning that day and hour, no one knows, not even the angels of heaven, nor the Son, but the Father only" (**Mat. 24:36**). I cannot guarantee the accuracy of any of the dates, as I found them on various websites. Nevertheless, I only aim to illustrate the frequency of these end-time predictions. For brevity, many have been excluded. Hippolytus, Sextus Africanus, and Irenaeus predicted that Jesus would return in 500. A Spanish monk believed the end would be on April 6th, 793. Many scholars and Pope Sylvester II anticipated the end on January 1st, 1000. When this did not occur, they revised it to January 1st, 1033

Sandro Botticelli predicted that the end of the world would occur in 1500. Michael Stifel, a mathematician, calculated that the Day of Judgment would begin at 8:00 AM on October 19, 1533. Johann Zimmerman believed that Jesus would return in 1694. Henry Archer used the 1,335 days mentioned in Daniel and predicted the end would come in 1700. Joanna Southcott, who believed she was pregnant with the Christ child, predicted that the world would end on December 25, 1814. John Wesley, the founder of the Methodist Church, believed that the millennium would start in 1836. Charles Russell, the first president of the Watchtower, thought it would arrive in 1874

Joseph Smith believed the end would come within 56 years of 1891. The Catholic Apostolic Church anticipated the end of time would occur in 1901. Herbert W. Armstrong expected it would happen before he died in 1986. A movement within the Seventh-day Adventist Church predicted the date to be October 1964. The "New World" magazine forecasted that the "final battle" was imminent in 1943. Hal Lindsey projected the end to be no later than 1988. Harold Camping declared that Christ's return would occur in 1994. John Hagee asserted that the coming of Christ was near and would begin with the assassination of Yitzhak Rabin in 1996

Many predicted that the year 2000 would be the end of the world, including the President of Yale University. Harold Camping forecasted that the end of time would occur on October 21, 2011. In 2000, one of the most publicized apocalyptic dates was 2012, which was based on the Mayan calendar. Mark Blitz asserted that Christ's return would begin on September 28, 2015. Ronald Weinland believed Christ would return in 2019

What do you notice about every one of the predictions mentioned in this article and the probable hundreds or thousands that were not mentioned? That's right; none of them came true. Surprisingly, many of these predictions came from Bible scholars who must have read verses that clearly refute the possibility of anyone knowing when that day will occur. **1 The. 5:2** states, "For you yourselves are fully aware that the day of the Lord will come like a thief in the night."

Even the book of Revelation indicates that mankind will not know the date of Christ's return: **Rev. 16:15**, "Behold, I am coming like a thief! Blessed is the one who stays awake, keeping his garments on, that he may not go about naked and be seen exposed!" In other words, don't be caught off-guard on that day. Live as if every day could be the day because it could be. Live every day in obedience and with joyful expectation of His return and pay no attention to end-time predictions.

Chapter 75
Wisdom over Health, Wealth, and Power

> "In that night God appeared to Solomon, and said to him, "Ask what I shall give you." And Solomon said to God, "You have shown great and steadfast love to David my father, and have made me king in his place. O Lord God, let your word to David my father be now fulfilled, for you have made me king over a people as numerous as the dust of the earth. Give me now wisdom and knowledge to go out and come in before this people, for who can govern this people of yours, which is so great?" (**2 Chr. 1:7-10**).

What would you honestly ask for if you had not read the verses above and God promised you anything your heart desires? Solomon was the second son of King David and Bathsheba. His path to being crowned king was fraught with challenges. A conspiracy led by his half-brother, Adonijah, and Joab, a general of David, forced Solomon to have them killed to secure his throne. This is where our story begins. Instead of requesting riches and glory, victory over his enemies, or even health, Solomon asks for something far more valuable for a king's success.

Most people would be tempted to ask for the things he did not. They believe money, health, and power will provide them security and freedom. While that isn't impossible, it is unlikely that these alone will lead to a fulfilling, comfortable, and worry-free life. In fact, it is precisely those things that strip a person of their reliance on God. Just look at the trajectory of the Western world since the 19th century. As medical advancements resulted in longer lifespans and economic policies created noticeably more wealth, God was pushed to the back seat and eventually expelled from the vehicle altogether. Who needs God when you have everything your heart desires, right

Solomon did the unthinkable by asking for only wisdom. What? He could have asked for anything but chose wisdom. "Whoopie-do, good luck with that," some might say, but if they seriously considered it, they would understand why. You see, with wisdom, you will know how to make money, live healthily, control your desires, and use everything at your disposal to improve yourself and those around you. Without wisdom, there's a big chance you might squander what you have in the future. Just think about how many people have earned a fortune only to lose it, or how many have won millions in the lottery and ended up penniless due to a lack of wisdom. Money doesn't guarantee good decisions, and neither does health ensure longevity.

Solomon understood the value of what he was asking for, and God was so impressed that he was given an abundance of it. **2 Chr. 1:11-12**,

> "God answered Solomon, "Because this was in your heart, and you have not asked for possessions, wealth, honor, or the life of those who hate you, and have not even asked for long life, but have asked for wisdom and knowledge for yourself that you may govern my people over whom I have made you king, wisdom and knowledge are granted to you. I will also give you riches, possessions, and honor, such as none of the kings had who were before you, and none after you shall have the like."

If you want God to grant you your requests, ask for what aligns with His will, and you will receive it (1Jo. 5:14). However, a word of caution: even wisdom, when not applied consistently and faithfully, can lead you down a dangerous path that may jeopardize your soul. Solomon had immense wisdom and success, but his carnal desires led him to act against God's will. He fell prey to the temptations that ensnared lesser men, allowing lust and greed to guide his actions. Instead of worshiping God, he constructed altars to foreign gods in Jerusalem.

The lesson is simple: keep striving to do what is good, for even wisdom from God does not guarantee that you will remain faithful, obedient, and happy. Remember the words of **1Co. 10:31** and do everything for the glory of God, keeping in mind the source of all that is good. **Jam. 1:17** says, "Every good gift and every perfect gift is from above, coming down from the Father of lights..." Do not use God's gifts to glorify the evil one. Utilize them wisely and resist the temptations that accompany them.

Chapter 76
Be Subject to the Governing Authorities

"Let every person be subject to the governing authorities. For there is no authority except from God, and those that exist have been instituted by God" (**Rom. 13:1**). Since we in the United States just had our midterm elections, I thought it would be a good time to write this article. In the months leading up to the election, all contenders attack each other, and the media cannot help but promote one candidate or another. One side criticizes the others' policies, the personal histories of their opponents, and their associations, seizing on any past mistakes. It doesn't take long for most rivalries to devolve into a chaotic shouting match of "He/she did this or that or said this or that terrible thing." What follows is nothing but ugliness and contempt for one another. Healthy, respectful debates seem to have been lost.

I have watched both ends of the political spectrum in the US criticize and despise the other side, whether they are fully aware or blissfully unaware of the toxic environment they are fostering. Politics revolves around wealth and power, appeasing sponsors, and ensuring one's base doesn't drift to the other side. They will do or say anything to secure those votes. That is politics, and whether we like it or not, it's a reality, both here and in every country that holds fair and free elections. Freedom of speech can be a harsh master, leading to statements that may be hurtful or inaccurate—another facet of politics. Both sides believe their candidate never lies and has only the best intentions, while viewing the other as laughable—a foolish liar with nothing to contribute. Regardless of the situation, we will cast our votes, and there will be a winner.

But what happens the day after the election chaos? What are we supposed to do until the next election cycle, where we can once again make our voices heard? As Christians, our ultimate authority is always the Bible, and when the government contradicts it, we should follow the Word of God, but that doesn't mean we should respond with violence. Use your voice, not your hands, when you disagree. Holding a different opinion, even one that opposes the government, is not necessarily against the law (as long as it isn't something like refusing to pay taxes or something similar). And while we're on the topic of taxes, let's quote our Savior.

> **Mar. 12:13-17**, "And they sent to him some of the Pharisees and some of the Herodians, to trap him in his talk. And they came and said to him, "Teacher, we know that you are true and do not care about anyone's opinion. For you are not swayed by appearances, but truly teach the way of God. Is it lawful to pay taxes to Caesar, or not? Should we pay them, or should we not?" But, knowing their hypocrisy, he said to them,
>
> "Why put me to the test? Bring me a denarius and let me look at it." And they brought one. And he said to them, "Whose likeness and inscription is this?" They said to him, "Caesar's." Jesus said to them, "Render to Caesar the things that are Caesar's, and to God the things that are God's." And they marveled at him."

Look, none of us enjoy parting with our hard-earned money for the IRS, but at the same time, we appreciate asphalt roads, electricity, a municipality, a police force, firefighters, hospitals, etc. So, I am an unwilling yet willing payer of my taxes. I value amenities, so I invest in them. Here's my perspective on obedience to authorities, drawn from the pages of the Bible, my ultimate authority. Get involved, vote, voice your concerns if you lose, and celebrate if you win. Regardless of your outcome this time, history shows it will shift. That's the essence of democracy. Critique the policies, but do so peacefully, always remembering that we represent the Creator God in all our actions. Respect those with differing opinions, and always express the love of Christ in all your communications.

Consider trying to win them to Christ instead of your political party. And the final word goes to God through His perfect Word. **Rom. 13:2-7,**

> "Therefore whoever resists the authorities resists what God has appointed, and those who resist will incur judgment. For rulers are not a terror to good conduct, but to bad. Would you have no

fear of the one who is in authority? Then do what is good, and you will receive his approval, for he is God's servant for your good. But if you do wrong, be afraid, for he does not bear the sword in vain. For he is the servant of God, an avenger who carries out God's wrath on the wrongdoer.

Therefore one must be in subjection, not only to avoid God's wrath but also for the sake of conscience. For because of this you also pay taxes, for the authorities are ministers of God, attending to this very thing. Pay to all what is owed to them: taxes to whom taxes are owed, revenue to whom revenue is owed, respect to whom respect is owed, honor to whom honor is owed."

Chapter 77
At the Bottom of the Ocean

"We who are strong have an obligation to bear with the failings of the weak, and not to please ourselves" (**Rom. 15:1**). In my humble opinion, this is one of the most significant weaknesses of the modern church. Let me explain what I mean with an example. I was a youth minister at a church many years ago. On more than one occasion, after some incident involving teens, I would hear the "mature" complain that young teens or immature Christians should not do certain things because the latter is a stumbling block to the former.

Instead of remembering that they, too, were once infant Christians, they complain that the youth are "causing problems in my faith." When people, especially teens, decide to obey the gospel and get baptized, we expect them to behave like fully mature Christians. We don't understand why they still act as they did before becoming Christians - as if baptism is the final step in a believer's maturation. When we read **1Pe. 2:2**, we begin to understand the process a little more, "Like newborn infants, long for the pure spiritual milk, that by it you may grow up into salvation." When a baby is born, does the mother leave it to fend for itself, find its own food, and learn the intricacies of life? Of course not.

The mother understands that the infant is now more than ever in need of her nurturing. Without the milk the baby "craves," as it is their life force, they would soon perish. The same applies to the infant Christian. Why do we study with them, leading them to the waters of baptism, only to abandon them from that moment on? This is when the evil one will viciously attack them. He knows they are still weak, wavering in their understanding. He realizes the foundation is still setting and that the best time to undo anything is before it hardens. He will not miss the opportunity to damage their spirituality. He will strike quickly and fiercely.

Instead of strengthening them with further study and words of encouragement, we play into Satan's hands and attack them, confusing them and driving a nail into their spiritual coffin. Even more tragically, when they stumble because of our actions, we fail to recognize our role and blame them for succumbing to their sinful nature. This is precisely what happens to weak Christians as well. They are scolded for their sinful actions and made to feel like pathetic rejects in the house of the righteously pious. At other times, the mature desire sermons and lessons tailored to their maturity level, disregarding the immature. They should simply concentrate and study harder. How ignorant are they that they cannot grasp a 401 lesson while still at a 101 level to use a university analogy concept?

In many cases, there is a reason for that. The "mature" individuals were left in a similar predicament when they were baptized-left to fend for themselves without a nurturing adult believer to feed them the Word of God and strengthen them in all things positive, including empathy. The writer of Hebrews has a word for them. **Heb 5:12**, "For though by this time you ought to be teachers, you need someone to teach you again the basics principles of the oracles of God." Nothing is more frustrating than a mature Christian who believes they possess all the spiritual wisdom in the world. Because they are so childish, everything revolves around them and their needs, to the detriment of the weaker brother or sister. They may be more mature than the infant Christian but are still far less so than they should be.

In our verse for the day, Paul wants them to understand that it is not a favor but rather an obligation to bear with the failings of the weak. If it is a blessing for someone to guide a wandering soul back to the light, how much punishment awaits one who causes another soul to wander? **Jam. 5:20** references bringing a sinner back, "let him know that whoever brings back a sinner from his wandering will save his soul from death and will cover a multitude of sins. **Mat. 18:6** references the danger of causing the weak to wander,

> "but whoever causes one of these little ones who believe in me to sin, it would be better for him to have a great millstone fastened around his neck and to be drowned in the depth of the sea."

Don't cause the weak to wander, or you may find yourself at the bottom of the ocean.

Chapter 78
Thank You, God, Thank You, Jesus

"For if we go on sinning deliberately after receiving the knowledge of the truth, there no longer remains a sacrifice for sins, but a fearful expectation of judgment, and a fury of fire that will consume the adversaries" (**Heb. 10:26-27**).

Those words are actually quite frightening. Some delusional individuals may claim to be sinless, but the rest of us recognize our fallen nature and tendency to sin. In fact, the Bible is quite clear on this matter. It does not suggest that we might be sinners; it states that we are sinners. Furthermore, it's not solely Adam's fault that we tend to sin – we share the blame. While we are not responsible for sin, we have the same choice as Adam and Eve in the Garden of Eden.

Although they were created in the image of God, they chose to be disobedient and eat from the tree of the knowledge of good and evil. The Bible states this in **Rom. 5:12**, "Therefore, just as sin came into the world through one man, and death through sin, and so death spread to all men because all sinned." Two things stand out to me in this verse. Firstly, sin entered the world not because Adam was sinful by nature but because, as I mentioned earlier, he had a choice and made the wrong one. Secondly, death spread to all men because all sinned, not just a few – ALL SINNED.

Rom. 3:23 states, "for all have sinned and fall short of the glory of God." This speaks of you and me, my friend – no exceptions. You know the delusional souls I mentioned earlier; the Bible has some choice words for them. **1Jo. 1:8** says, "If we say we have no sin, we deceive ourselves, and the truth is not in us." We must admit we sin to do something about it. No one who claims they are not doing anything wrong will take steps to correct it. Moreover, when the writer of Hebrews says, "If we go on sinning deliberately," he might as well have said, "WHEN we go on sinning."

It's safe to assume that everyone will occasionally sin deliberately. "Oh, I try not to," you might say, but even that is an admission of guilt. "Well, I don't murder, steal, or cheat," you may counter, yet those are obvious sins. I'm not just referring to those; I mean also the things we don't typically see as sinful. Gossiping, slandering someone, falsely accusing an individual of something they didn't do, or taking a single pen from a desk is also a deliberate sin. Even the infamous "white lie" is technically a sin. Nowhere in the Bible does it say that lying is acceptable to spare a child's feelings or to let someone off the hook when breaking up with them.

I know it seems harsh, but it is what it is. Most people will quickly lose their temper in a road rage incident or yell profanity when someone does something they consider heinous. They indulge in life's vices—greed, lust, envy, gluttony, and sloth—to satisfy their desires without a second thought. One would hope this does not apply to Christians, but sadly, I must say there are undoubtedly many who engage in them. The title "son or daughter of God" does not automatically eliminate our tendency to succumb to our carnal desires at times.

Sinning after we've come to know the truth is an affront to God. The only just punishment for our actions is eternal banishment. But, thank God, we have an advocate pleading our case before the Creator. **1Jo. 2:1**,

> "My little children, I am writing these things to you so that you may not sin. But if anyone does sin, we have an advocate with the Father, Jesus Christ the righteous.

In the very next verse, we read how He accomplishes that for us, "He is the propitiation for our sins, and not for ours only but also for the sins of the whole world" (**1Jo. 1:22.**). That doesn't mean we should continue sinning; instead, it acknowledges that even though our fallen, sinful nature may cause us trouble from time to time, we have someone in our corner pleading our case. Thanks to Him, we will not receive the punishment we deserve if we repent. Thank you, God, for Jesus, and thank you, Jesus, for appeasing God.

Chapter 79
Correcting an Opponent with Gentleness

"And the Lord's servant must not be quarrelsome but kind to everyone, able to teach, patiently enduring evil, correcting his opponents with gentleness. God may perhaps grant them repentance leading to a knowledge of the truth...." (**2Ti. 2:24-25**).

Do you find it challenging when you meet someone, whether a stranger or a friend, who begins to question the Bible or your faith? Do they frustrate you when they raise a point that is entirely out of context to prove something invalid from the outset? In their view, they are making their argument so clear that you will have no choice but to agree with them and reject this whole "Jesus thing."

It is difficult to tolerate fools, especially when they refuse to listen to anything but the incoherent babble rattling around in their empty heads. Sometimes, the only way to break through to their thick skulls is to match their volume and aggression, demonstrating that you are not a coward who will back down even a little. I realize that sounds harsh, but my point is that many Christians behave this way when confronted by someone who questions them with a degree of hostility. Of course, that isn't the best response and will only result in hurt feelings and anger. Some time ago, I came across a gentleman who was trying my patience, questioning my intelligence for believing in the "man upstairs" and saying that I believe in a book that contradicts itself.

I remained calm, reciting **2Ti. 2:24-25** to myself, but my peaceful demeanor only fueled his anger. At this point, he threw his figurative punch – the one that would deliver the winning blow and knock me out of the verbal dispute. I knew he was preparing for that because he suddenly lowered the volume of his voice, which had become progressively louder, and smirked like someone with an undeniable surprise of epic proportions. He was already celebrating his grand victory when he asked me to explain the difference between John's baptism and Jesus's. Of course, he could not leave it there, so he added, "If John's baptism was all that was needed, Christ's baptism was not needed." He paused for effect before smugly continuing, "And if Christ's baptism is the correct one, then everyone who John baptized was baptized for no reason since they are lost."

The smirk had transformed into a smile, as he believed he had caught me. I was going to have to agree with him, and then I would be on my way to freedom from the constraints of the Bible and all its nonsense. Of course, this man's attitude is prevalent today, and dare I say, always has been among "clever-in-their-own-mind" ignorant debaters. Most have never read more than one or two Bible verses, or they have drawn conclusions from others who may have done just a bit more reading. By this point, I was thoroughly annoyed but realized that when aggression meets aggression, nothing positive comes from it. I breathed, smiled politely, and said, "Both are saved." He glared at me furiously and shot back, "Explain!"

I continued, "The only differences between the two baptisms are Christ and the Holy Spirit. John baptized for the repentance of sin and the recognition of the coming Savior, whereas Christ's baptism is done in His name and allows one to receive the gift of the Holy Spirit. John's baptism is pre-resurrection, while Christ's is post-resurrection." I then read two verses to prove my point. **Mar. 1:4**, "John appeared, baptizing in the wilderness and proclaiming a baptism of repentance for the forgiveness of sins," and **Act. 2:38**,

> "And Peter said to them, "Repent and be baptized every one of you in the name of Jesus Christ for the forgiveness of your sins, and you will receive the gift of the Holy Spirit."

He was not too happy at that point, but after some more discussion, we became friends, and later, I was fortunate enough to study with him. For the record, Christ's baptism is ultimately superior to John's precisely because the latter did not provide the Holy Spirit. **Act. 19:2-5**,

> "And he said to them <disciples at Ephesus>, "Did you receive the Holy Spirit when you believed?" And they said, "No, we have not even heard that there is a Holy Spirit." And he said, "Into what

then were you baptized?" They said, "Into John's baptism." And Paul said, "John baptized with the baptism of repentance, telling the people to believe in the one who was to come after him, that is, Jesus." On hearing this, they were baptized in the name of the Lord Jesus.

Chapter 80
Deny, Carry, Follow

"And calling the crowd to Him with His disciples, He said to them, 'If anyone would come after Me, let him deny himself and take up his cross and follow Me" (**Mar. 8:34**). I wonder how many people have read this and noticed something strange about Jesus' words. The conditional statement that starts with "If" is followed by three imperatives: "deny himself," "take up his cross," and "follow me." You might say this makes perfect sense, but remove the second and third imperatives and read it again: "If anyone would come after me" (follow me), "he must take up his cross and follow me." It seems redundant, but before jumping to conclusions, let's examine what Jesus says more closely. He begins with, "If anyone would come after me," which means being counted as a disciple.

Why would anyone want to do that, anyway? Let's read **Joh. 14:6-7** to find out: "Jesus said to him (Thomas), 'I am the way, and the truth, and the life. No one comes to the Father except through me.'" Those willing to follow Jesus understand that He is the only way to heaven. There is no person, alternative religion, teaching, idea, or ideology that can secure us a place in heaven. Therefore, it follows that Jesus is expressing a conditional statement to people who have heard Him and are wondering what to do next. Always remember the duality of scripture and how the message applies to us.

The first thing we must do is deny ourselves. That may seem odd to the uninitiated, but it doesn't mean we should say, "I am not me." Instead, we should deny our claim to the world and its possessions. You see, before we can truly follow Jesus, we need to understand what that entails. An easy way of describing that is **Mat. 6:24**,

> "No one can serve two masters, for either he will hate the one and love the other, or he will be devoted to the one and despise the other. You cannot serve God and money."

Our carnal selves desire to sin, and we must deny that part of us. Furthermore, this will not be easy. The devil will not relinquish a lost soul without a struggle.

The second thing we must do is take up our cross. But what does that really mean? It's not as if there's a wooden cross by our front door that we need to hoist and carry through the streets of our town. I would guess Jesus really captured the crowd's attention when He said those words, as that would typically lead to a crucifixion. That would have been just as frightening as what Jesus said in **Joh. 12:25**, "Whoever loves his life loses it, and whoever hates his life in this world will keep it for eternal life." Fortunately, Jesus does not refer to a physical cross or death. This point emphasizes the idea of denying oneself.

Once we have done that, we must commit to it by putting those things aside, or as **Gal. 5:24** succinctly states, "And those who belong to Christ Jesus have crucified the flesh with its passions and desires." In other words, we cannot just give it lip service by denying it; we must truly put to death the things of the world. The final aspect is to follow Jesus. The first "follow" was directed at those who wish to follow, while this "follow" refers to the action taken when we have denied ourselves and are carrying our cross. Since He is the Good Shepherd, we must follow Him with the same loyalty and reliance as a sheep.

We have already read that Jesus is the way (**Joh. 14:6**), so the only way to reach heaven is by actively following Him. This means we will adhere to His commands and follow His example. We will walk with him as we are told to do in **1Jo. 2:6**, "Whoever says he abides in him ought to walk in the same way in which he walked." If Christians would follow Jesus with the same zeal they exhibit for their favorite sports team, actor, singer, or television show series.

Chapter 81
The Resurrection Was No Hoax

The other day, I was speaking to a young lady who questioned the resurrection of Jesus. "Other than the first four books of the Bible, you have no proof." Well, mentioning the "First four books" gave her knowledge of the Bible away, so I asked her if she had ever read it. She said she had and that she actually carried it in her car somewhere. After she retrieved it, I realized someone had given her a New Testament-only Bible, so it was clear why she thought the Gospels were the first four books. I asked if she would meet me at the church the following day, and she agreed. As arranged, I met with her the next day in my office.

I started by explaining the difference between the two testaments and then asked if she was aware of any other resurrections in the Bible. "I have skimmed the book and don't think I saw any," she replied. Having done some research the previous night, I showed her that there were references to several resurrections. They are mentioned in the Bible in **1Ki. 17:17–24**, where Elijah raised the widow's son; **2Ki. 4:32–37**, where Elisha raised a child; **2Ki. 13:20–21**, where a dead man whose body touched that of Elisha was restored; **Mat. 27:52–53**, where tombs were opened, and the bodies of saints were raised; **Mar. 5:35–43**, where Jesus raised Jairus's daughter, **Luk. 7:11–17**, where Jesus restored the widow's son, **Joh. 11:39–44**, where Jesus raised Lazarus; **Act. 9:40**, where Peter raised Tabitha, and in **Act. 20:9-10**, where Paul raised Eutychus

That intrigued the young lady, and she began to listen intently as I spoke about a book I had read titled "Who Moved the Stone" by Frank Morrison. We read a few excerpts, and then, with an air of excitement, we returned to the question at hand: "Proof of the resurrection of Jesus." Before proceeding, I asked her, "Do you know who invented penicillin?" After some prompting, she recalled and said, "Alexander Fleming." "Good, but how do you know that?" She looked puzzled and replied, "I read it in books."

I continued my questions, "You read it, but you weren't there yourself, right?" "Duh, of course not!" she replied snarkily. "Okay, just remember that as we go forward because you're saying you trust the eyewitnesses from that time." I will provide all the internal evidence for the Resurrection of Jesus, witnessed by those who were there or knew the witnesses. Moreover, I will prove to you another day that the Bible is authentic. If I can do that, will you then admit that the Resurrection of Jesus actually happened and is not a fanciful fable created by deluded people who call themselves Christians?" "I think I would, but we'll see." "Good enough for me," I replied. Then, I presented her with the evidence for Christ's Resurrection.

The resurrected Jesus is documented as appearing in Judea (**Mat. 28:9; Luk. 24:31, 36**) and Galilee (**Mat. 28:16-20; Joh. 21:1-23**), in towns (**Luk. 24:36**) and in the countryside (**Luk. 24:15**), indoors (**Luk. 24:36**) and outdoors (**Mat. 28:9, 16; Luk. 24:15; Joh. 21:1-23**), in the morning (**Joh. 21:1-23**) and in the evening (**Luk. 24:29, 36; Joh. 20:19**), by prior appointment (**Mat. 28:16**) and without prior appointment (**Mat. 28:9; Luk. 24:15, 34, 36; Joh. 21:1-23**), close by (**Mat. 28:9, 19; Luk. 24:15, 36; Joh. 21:9-23**) and distant (**Joh. 21:4-8**), on a hill (**Mat. 28:16**) and by a lake (**Joh. 21:4**), to groups of men (**Joh. 21:2; 1Co. 15:5, 7**) and groups of women (**Mat. 28:9**), to individuals (**Luk. 24:34; 1Co. 15:5, 7-8**) and groups of up to five hundred (**1Co. 15:6**), sitting (**Joh 21:15** implied), standing (**Jn 21:4**), walking (**Luk 24:15; Joh 21:20-22**), eating (**Luk 24:43; Jn 21:15**), and always talking (**Mat 28:9-10, 18-20; Luk 24:17-30, 36-49; Joh. 20:15-17, 19-29; 21:6-22**). Courtesy of Peter Williams. That was enough for her; she has returned several times to study the Bible with me.

Chapter 82
My First and Foremost Love

"...You shall love the Lord your God with all your heart and with all your soul and with all your mind" (**Mat. 22:37**).

Who is the most important love of your life? I am blessed with a wonderful wife who stood by my side when I was critically ill. She had to do everything for me – things no one should have to do. We have never fought, never exchanged hurtful words, never spoken ill of each other, and we spend nearly every hour of every day together. She has my heart. I have a daughter who is fiercely protective of her "Daddy." If you hurt me, she will come unglued. She is beautiful and sharp as a tack. She has my heart. My son-in-law is a good man and an exceptional father. This relatively new addition to the family also has my heart.

My oldest son is my verbal sparring partner. We argue about taxes, politics, world affairs, and anything else we can think of, but once it's over, we move on with a hug. He would lie down behind me when I was too sick to move, using his body warmth to heat me. He was 17 years old at the time. He has my heart. My youngest son is a Marine reservist, and I couldn't be prouder. He is focused and exemplifies the Marine's code of conduct: honor, courage, and commitment. He is everything I wish I had been at that age. He has my heart, too. My family (including Mel's) all have my heart. My church family holds a special place in my life as well. They are encouraging, annoying, and lovable (did I mention annoying?). They have my heart.

I could go on, but I think you get the point. If you know me, you might ask the obvious question now: why have I left two people out? This was intentional because they are, well, quite special. They are my two granddaughters, the Butterfly Princess and the Unicorn Princess. They are cute, wonderful, beautiful, amazing, lovable, kind, intelligent, courageous, and every other positive descriptor you can imagine. They have my heart. Oh, they definitely have my heart. Each of the aforementioned has a unique type and depth of love, but which is the most important love of my life.

None of them, actually. That's right, not my wife, kids, grandkids, family, friends, or anyone else on earth can compare to my greatest love – The Lord. As much as I love everyone, even the most special of them pales compared to my love for the Almighty. The best part is they are all well aware of it and happy for me. I know their first love is God as well. He is not only my creator, who knew me before my birth (**Jer. 1:5**, "Before I formed you in the womb I knew you..."), but all the loves of my life are gifts from Him. I am acutely aware that nothing I cherish would have meaning without the God of the universe, the creator and sustainer of life.

I love Him first and foremost because He loved me first (**1Jo. 4:19**) and sent His perfect Son to be the unblemished Lamb, the propitiation for my sinful nature. My love for God does not diminish my love for those mentioned earlier; rather, it frees me to love them as much as I do. Perhaps more than most, I know how little I deserve His unconditional love. I am grateful that He loved me when I was not worth the effort and thankful for His grace and mercy. I am incredibly grateful for the gift of His Son, who paved the way for my hope of an eternity in heaven.

Joh. 3:16, "For God so loved the world that he gave his only Son, that whoever believes in him should not perish but have eternal life." I deserve the worst, yet His love gives me the best. How could He then not be my life's first and foremost love?

Chapter 83
Continue in What You Have Learned

> "But as for you, continue in what you have learned and have firmly believed, knowing from whom you learned it and how from childhood you have been acquainted with the sacred writings, which can make you wise for salvation through faith in Christ Jesus" (**2Ti. 3:14-15**).

Most Christians know the following verses, and many can recite them from memory,

> "All Scripture is breathed out by God and profitable for teaching, for reproof, for correction, and for training in righteousness, that the man of God may be complete, equipped for every good work" (**2Ti. 3:16-17**).

Still, few edify using the two aforementioned passages. Paul is writing to Timothy to encourage him to continue what he has learned, likely from his mother, grandmother, and Paul himself.

However, I want to apply this to the present. If Paul spoke those words to you, how would they resonate in your life? Did a parent or grandparent teach you the scriptures when you were young? Did a favorite aunt, uncle, cousin, or friend, or did you learn it in church? Were you taught at all? Let's assume someone taught you and that you developed a growing understanding as you aged. You were fortunate, my friend, but will you continue in what you have learned, or will you abandon it for the lies and false promises of the world? **Pro. 1:8** says, "Hear, my son, your father's instruction, and forsake not your mother's teaching...." Will you waste their efforts to teach you God's truths?

If you were not taught the scriptures but discovered them on your own and are therefore considered "self-taught," the same applies to you. Fortunately, the Bible does not require a teacher to be understood. All it takes is an open mind and the willingness to accept its instruction in obedience. Either way, the question above is relevant to you as well. One of my all-time favorite verses (and one I probably use more than any other) is **Jos. 1:8,**

> "This Book of the Law shall not depart from your mouth, but you shall meditate on it day and night, so that you may be careful to do according to all that is written in it. For then you will make your way prosperous, and then you will have good success."

I love that particular verse because it is as relevant today as it was then and offers some of the best advice anyone can receive. Many people raised with the teachings of the Bible may feel less passion by the time they reach adulthood compared to those who have recently discovered their salvation within its pages. This tendency is almost human nature; the longer we engage in a particular relationship, the easier it becomes to feel bored, worn out, or even disenchanted by it. In such moments, the words of Paul should resonate with one's heart and rejuvenate one's spirit. Unfortunately, verses like this are often overlooked in favor of more prominent ones because there is wisdom in every word of the Bible, not just in the verses we consider "pithy nuggets."

The very real danger is that these teachings may give way to the false teachings of the world or self-centered preachers and teachers. You will note that Paul states staying the course will make you "wise for salvation through faith in Christ Jesus." Someone once said, "...salvation lies not in the Scriptures themselves, but only as they are properly understood to point to Christ. For Paul, salvation is always through faith in Christ Jesus." The more you study the word, the clearer its meaning becomes, and the more your wisdom regarding your salvation grows. The Bible is a source of incredible knowledge—knowledge that won't make you famous, secure a world-class, high-paying job, or anything like that (although developing the qualities found in the Bible certainly won't hurt you in those respects), but rather the knowledge that transcends earthly matters.

The knowledge, or rather, the wisdom you gain from the Good Book, will prepare you for the ultimate success—an eternity in heaven. However, be warned: all the promises of God, culminating in the hope of salvation for all who love Him and are obedient, will be granted only to those who continue in what they have learned, whether from childhood or just last month. While doing so will not ensure a life free of trials, its conclusion will be better than ever imagined. **1Co.2:9**, "But, as it is written, "What no eye has seen, nor ear heard, nor the heart of man imagined, what God has prepared for those who love him."

Chapter 84
Like a Superhero but More Powerful

"What then shall we say to these things? If God is for us, who can be against us? He who did not spare His own Son but gave Him up for us all, how will He not also with Him graciously give us all things?" (**Rom. 8:31-32**).

These two verses, spoken by the Apostle Paul to the Roman church and, by extension, to us, should encourage us during our hardships. When God is for us, it means we have met the requirements outlined in His Word to be considered adopted children and heirs of the fortune that is everlasting life. God's power is at our disposal when we walk in obedience—how comforting is that?

Less comforting, perhaps, is the fact that we will encounter those trials and tribulations more frequently than we realize. Unfortunately, some churches propagate a false notion that we are exempt from the devil's attacks once we have accepted Christ through baptism. I came across a quote taken out of context to support that claim. **Mat. 6:13** states, "And lead us not into temptation, but deliver us from evil." It might be clearer to express it as "deliver us from the temptations of the evil one," but more on that later. Suffice it to say that the individual's interpretation was overly literal for the context – highlighting the ever-present danger of a superficial reading of the scriptures.

No Christian should doubt that temptations, trials, and hardships will pursue us throughout the marathon of a life lived in obedience to God. In fact, we are promised that in **Joh. 15:18-20**,

> "If the world hates you, know that it has hated me before it hated you. If you were of the world, the world would love you as its own; but because you are not of the world, but I chose you out of the world, therefore the world hates you. Remember the word that I said to you: 'A servant is not greater than his master.' If they persecuted me, they will also persecute you."

The same promise is found in **2Ti. 3:12**, "Indeed, all who desire to live a godly life in Christ Jesus will be persecuted." However, we need not fear the challenges we are sure to encounter, as we have the power of the Creator on our side. We receive another comforting message in **Php. 4:13**: "I can do all things through him who strengthens me."

Even when the trial's outcome brings tribulation in the form of disease or grief, we have the power to hold onto the faith that gives us the courage to persevere. That faith, unwavering in its loyalty, assures us that even during these hardships, we are not being defeated but are growing. **Rom. 5:3-5**,

> "Not only that, but we rejoice in our sufferings, knowing that suffering produces endurance, and endurance produces character, and character produces hope, and hope does not put us to shame because God's love has been poured into our hearts through the Holy Spirit who has been given to us."

What the world sees as utter despair and defeat, we see as the opportunity to grow in the promise of a hope of a better forever.

Our time on earth may be filled with suffering and pain, whether in the short term or long term, but in either case, we have a goal that drives us through those times and triumphantly towards a future where tears, pain, and suffering no longer exist. **2Co. 4:16-18**,

> "So we do not lose heart. Though our outer self is wasting away, our inner self is being renewed day by day. For this light momentary affliction is preparing for us an eternal weight of glory beyond all comparison, as we look not to the things that are seen but to the things that are unseen. For the things that are seen are transient, but the things that are unseen are eternal."

We see that the world is incapable of recognizing Godly hope. Therefore, man cannot defeat us, hardships cannot force us to our knees, and the devil is powerless to destroy our hope. We are, therefore, invincible, like a superhero, but even more powerful since we have the unlimited power of God on our side.

Chapter 85
Encouraged Today, Doomed Tomorrow

> "Him we proclaim, warning everyone and teaching everyone with all wisdom, that we may present everyone mature in Christ. For this I toil, struggling with all his energy that he powerfully works within me" (**Col. 1:28-29**).

Paul has just discussed the service and stewardship God has entrusted to him. He continues this theme by highlighting two crucial aspects of his ministry of proclamation: warning and teaching everyone. Today, we will focus on the first aspect. He mentions that he and his colleagues were warning everyone, but what does he mean by that? In recent years, preaching the Word of God has become a politically correct, never-step-on-toes affair—full of empty rhetoric with little real spiritual substance.

The "Good News" is not preached as much as everyone in the audience is made to feel welcome and "safe." To achieve this, their feelings are considered, and care is taken not to upset them. Scriptures, if mentioned at all during what is more of a motivational speech than anything else, are carefully selected to encourage and uplift. Of course, there's nothing wrong with that since the message of Christ is ultimately Good News. Take **Joh. 3:16-17**, the well-known and arguably most loved scripture in the entire Bible:

> "For God so loved the world, that he gave his only Son, that whoever believes in him should not perish but have eternal life. For God did not send his Son into the world to condemn the world, but in order that the world might be saved through him."

The Bible is filled with verses like these for a good reason—the message is about God's love and the opportunity Christ provided for the Creator's most prized possession. However, and this is a significant "however," there is more to the story than that. Read **Joh. 3:18**, and the complete truth is revealed, "Whoever believes in him is not condemned, but whoever does not believe is condemned already, because he has not believed in the name of the only Son of God." One can also read **Rom. 3:23**, "for all have sinned and fall short of the glory of God," followed by Rom. **6:23**, "For the wages of sin is death...." Words of encouragement accompany both Roman passages. However, the point is that the message needs to include more than just placatory biblical tidbits.

There must be warnings, sometimes dire, for man to make the most informed decision regarding his future. Take, for instance, **Act. 20:19**,

> "I know that after my departure, fierce wolves will come in among you, not sparing the flock, and from among your own selves will arise men speaking twisted things, to draw away the disciples after them."

Paul wanted the readers of Acts to be aware of the dangers of false teachers. An even more severe warning is found in the Book of Hebrews. **Heb. 6:4-6**,

> "For it is impossible, in the case of those who have once been enlightened, who have tasted the heavenly gift, and have shared in the Holy Spirit, and have tasted the goodness of the word of God and the powers of the age to come, and then have fallen away, to restore them again to repentance, since they are crucifying once again the Son of God to their own harm and holding him up to contempt."

Not every sermon or Bible lesson needs to be all "doom and gloom," especially since we recognize that the overarching theme of the Bible, particularly the New Testament, is the assured hope of the future glory of heaven. However, as Paul emphasizes, we would be remiss to ignore those warnings just to please the hearers' emotional desires. We certainly do not want to fall into the category of the teacher mentioned in **2Ti. 4:3**,

> "For the time is coming when people will not endure sound teaching, but having itching ears, they will accumulate for themselves teachers to suit their own passions...."

The good news is that Jesus died for us; the bad news is that we are flawed beings who must be cautioned about what could personally undermine His sacrifice for us. The role of a teacher or preacher is to present the whole scriptures to the audience, not just the "feel-good" parts that may uplift them emotionally today but could spell doom for them tomorrow.

Chapter 86
Church Leaders Don't Own You

"And he is the head of the body, the church. He is the beginning, the firstborn from the dead, that in everything he might be preeminent" (**Col. 1:18**). A close friend and sister in Christ raised an excellent question last week: "Are a church's congregants subject to its leader's totalitarian authority?" She had been reflecting on her somewhat challenging past in a denominational church where the pastor demanded unwavering obedience and acted like a lord over "his people." Even a casual examination of churches worldwide, especially some megachurches, reveals this issue as an ongoing, though unscriptural, reality. Both men and women dominate the stage and behave as if their leadership roles grant them the authority to dictate absolutely everything to an often unsuspecting following.

Heb. 13:17 is then cited to qualify their god-like status before a crowd of adoring, hypnotized, or fearful congregants – "Obey your leaders and submit to them..." Thousands unfamiliar with the scriptures often credit the leader(s) with an authority they do not possess or deserve. There is no doubt that a church requires a leadership structure that will grow alongside its population, and it is also clear that leaders deserve the respect their positions warrant. However, let's be very clear: respect should never translate into blind loyalty. If any minister begins to demand anything beyond what the scriptures allow, the congregation should flee as quickly as possible.

The preacher is not in charge; the elders are in charge; the deacons are not in charge; the teachers are not in charge—Christ is. No man holds the title "Head of the church." That title and all its authority belong solely to Jesus Christ. Leadership is a vital component in the mechanism of obedience to the Scriptures, and sound, humble leaders are a blessing to the scriptural health and accuracy of the church. Many Scriptures, like **1Pe. 5:1-2** and **1Th. 5:12** clearly indicates that church leadership is necessary for successful growth, but no verse in the Bible permits any leader to lord over the people. In fact, the Bible demands quite the opposite in **1Pe. 5:3**, "not domineering (lording) over those in your charge, but being examples to the flock."

When a leader views himself as anything more than a humble, undeserving servant of Christ, his leadership is rendered null and void and should be replaced. What kind of example does a leader set who demands total allegiance to himself rather than the scriptures? Certainly not one who strives to emulate the Master, Christ Jesus. His example is one of servanthood: **Mat. 20:28**, "...even as the Son of Man came not to be served but to serve, and to give his life as a ransom for many." Jesus secured our loyalty through His perfect example and through His blood, not through His elevated position, which was bestowed upon Him by the Father: **Mat. 28:18**, "And Jesus came and said to them, "All authority in heaven and on earth has been given to me.'"

If the great "**I Am**" (**Joh. 8:58**) did not take it upon Himself to dominate the sheep, what gives man the right to do so? I am a pulpit minister, not a god. I do not own the flock. Christ's flock has been entrusted to my care to lead away from destruction and toward salvation through doctrinally sound preaching and teaching. Elders, too, are to shepherd the flock with the love and care of Christ, as they are clearly directed to do in verses like **1Pe. 5:2**, "shepherd the flock of God that is among you, exercising oversight...."

Do not allow a leader to confer more authority to himself than permitted. And never believe for a second that he owns any part of you... he does not. Respect your church leaders, but do not surrender your soul to them. They did not pay the price for it; Christ did: **1Co. 6:20**, "for you were bought with a price. So glorify God in your body."

Chapter 87
Just.Don't.Give.Up.

"...fear not, for I am with you; be not dismayed, for I am your God; I will strengthen you, I will help you, I will uphold you with my righteous right hand." (**Isa. 41:10**). Anyone who lives long enough will experience loss, but some losses are far worse than others. Most people are fortunate to have never faced a hurricane, tornado, earthquake, snowstorm, flood, or any other natural disaster. They have never had to stand where their home once stood and wonder, "Why?" or "What's next?" They have not searched through the rubble for priceless photos and keepsakes that served as treasured memories of days gone by.

They have not been overwhelmed by fear while searching for a pet or someone dear to them whom they last saw before the disaster struck. Most people have not experienced the searing pain of feeling the life drain from their bodies when they open their front door to find two heavy-hearted military officers in full dress uniforms standing there. They have not had to bury a loved one who chose to enlist in our military and then paid the ultimate price for others' safety. Most people have not had a police or firefighter chaplain standing at their door, informing them that their loved one was killed in the line of duty.

Most people have not had to endure the indescribable anguish of holding their stillborn baby in their arms—a child who will never breathe on its own, never say "Mommy," and never run around like toddlers do. Most people will not suffer the unbearable pain of burying a child whose life was tragically cut short. Most people have not felt the profound sorrow of standing at the grave of a loved one lost to a terrible illness, asking, "Why, God?" Most people will not confront such overwhelming grief that living no longer seems worthwhile. They will not spend days, months, years, and even decades waiting for the pain to return and the loss to be felt all over again, and again, and again.

Losing material possessions such as heirlooms, our homes, jobs, vehicles, and even friendships is challenging to endure. However, losing a loved one whom we will never see, hug, or kiss again is far more challenging. That kind of loss often leaves more questions than answers, and the wound may never heal completely. It's hard to understand why we must suffer so deeply in our lives, but the truth is that we will face tremendous loss at some point. I wish I could share today's verse with everyone who has experienced such suffering. I long to convey it in a way that helps them realize they are not alone during those times.

If that is you, know this: God is always there, strengthening you in your darkest hours, holding you up when you are too weak to stand, and carrying you emotionally when your energy reserves are completely spent. When words all but escape you, close your eyes and look up, and He will hear the thoughts you cannot express. He is with you when you stand where your house once was, when you hold the baby who is already in Paradise, when you stand at your child's grave, and at every other moment when a tragic event has stolen your joy. God is with you when you are at your wit's end, when you feel like life no longer holds meaning, and when giving up seems like the only path left.

He is there to comfort you, to strengthen you through your grief, and to instill hope in your seemingly hopeless situation. No matter how dark your current circumstances may appear, know that the Light of the world will soon dispel the darkness with the promise of tomorrow. Trust in Him, and together, even the worst tragedies in life can be overcome. **Heb. 13:5**, "...I will never leave you nor forsake you...." God is there, waiting for you to reach out to Him so He can provide comfort. Please call on Him and allow Him to help you right now. JUST.DON'T.GIVE.UP.

Chapter 88
When God Calls

"Now the Lord said to Abram, 'Go from your country and your kindred and your father's house to the land that I will show you" (**Gen. 12:1**). Have you ever found yourself at a crossroads, needing to decide what to do next? You might feel as though God is calling you to a ministry, yet at the same time, it can feel overwhelming. You want to obey, but you're not entirely sure it is God's will for you. Perhaps your desire is so strong that it blinds you to the reality that it might not be His will for your life. It's possible that your longing is so intense that you cannot hear Him cautioning you against moving forward.

However, after much prayer and soul-searching, you may feel completely confident that it is time to take a risk and follow God's plan for your life, daunting as it may be. When that happens, regardless of how certain you feel, those around you might not share your enthusiasm, and you may find yourself beginning your new journey alone. A friend of mine is moving to another state for a year to learn the skills needed to assist those in the community who have experienced or are currently experiencing abuse and/or addiction. This message is for her and for anyone at a similar crossroads in their life.

Choosing to venture out and blaze a new path is never easy. Family and friends may not fully understand your desire, and some may not offer their support. I suppose you can't blame them, as it is understandably difficult to fully embrace a vision you aren't personally connected to. However, the Bible is filled with examples of men and women who followed God's will, even when it must have seemed crazy to those around them. Take Noah, for instance. **Gen. 6:13-14**,

> "And God said to Noah, 'I have determined to make an end of all flesh, for the earth is filled with violence through them. Behold, I will destroy them with the earth. Make yourself an ark of gopher

wood. Make rooms in the ark and cover it inside and out with pitch."

Can you imagine his family when he told them what he was about to undertake – in his advanced years? What did his neighbors think as he slaved away, building a massive boat in his backyard?

How many family members and friends shared his vision? How many thought this man had lost his mind in his old age? And what about Abraham? How many people closely acquainted with him would have said, "Sure, Abraham. The voice you heard was God speaking to you. Go ahead, pack the camels, load up your family, and just head out until God says, Stop!" I would think not many. Perhaps you have done something similar and faced resistance from well-meaning friends and family who don't want to see you get hurt. Sometimes, they might instill just enough doubt in your mind to make you pause and reflect on your decision – which is OK.

Praying more and reassuring yourself of God's will for your life is never wrong, no matter how many people might think otherwise. It's better to wait a day for clarity than to act too hastily. However, when you are certain, you will feel powerfully drawn to your new path, emboldened by the courage that faith in God provides. You may also discover that some family and friends support your latest endeavor, even if they don't fully understand it. God did not place the vision in their hearts, but they trust that you are acting in good faith and with His blessing, wishing you well and praying for your journey to be productive and free of obstacles. Just remember, Satan does not want you to succeed, so anticipate challenges along the way.

Remember, God is infinitely more powerful than the devil; anything is possible with Christ in your corner. **Php. 4:13** states, "I can do all things through him who strengthens me." Take that step into the unknown with unwavering faith. Face and overcome the obstacles that will undoubtedly arise before you with fierce determination. Allow Him to guide you through the indwelling of the Holy Spirit and become a better version of yourself—a more exemplary Christian who can serve as a role model for others facing similar crossroads in their lives. **Jos. 1:9** says, "...Be strong and courageous. Do not be frightened, and do not be dismayed, for the Lord your God is with you wherever you go."

Chapter 89
The Secret Message on Your Tombstone

"I have fought the good fight, I have finished the race, I have kept the faith" (**2Ti. 4:7**). They say that man's greatest fear is death. Except for those who are still alive when Jesus returns, every single person who is born will eventually face death. People spend excessive amounts of time and money trying to postpone their end, but ultimately, they, too, will die. About 150,000 people die each day. Death is inevitable for everyone, from the poorest to the wealthiest person on Earth. No deal can be made with death.

I have witnessed numerous people die. Ministers encounter death many times throughout their lives. Not as frequently as, let's say, a doctor, but we do see more than we would like as part of our ministerial duties. People occasionally ask us to officiate a funeral for their loved ones. Of course, it is a privilege to be invited to participate in the memorial for someone who has passed on, and we seldom decline the opportunity. At times, we stand before grieving family and friends, confidently praising the life of a believer, assured that he or she is in paradise, awaiting the return of Jesus. Other times, we are less certain, so we carefully choose our words about their afterlife.

There are also times when we are quite certain that the final destination will not be what God intended for the deceased, yet we officiate, nonetheless. Every person deserves a moment for family and friends to say their final goodbyes. The point is this: some will be in a good place, and others will not, as we clearly read in **Luk. 16:22-23**,

> "The poor man died and was carried by the angels to Abraham's side. The rich man also died and was buried, and in Hades, being in torment, he lifted his eyes and saw Abraham far off and Lazarus at his side."

Every gravestone or monument represents a soul that has departed from this life and is now experiencing one of those two places – paradise or torment.

When I see a graveyard, I sometimes reflect on who will be raised and called to an eternity of heavenly bliss and who will not. What is the secret message on the tombstone? Heaven-bound or hell-bound? Just as our eventual demise is inevitable, so is the destination based on how we live. Neither heaven nor hell was imprinted on your heart the day you were born. Your future was not decided for you, as if you had absolutely no control over it. From the moment you understand the consequences of sin, you begin to determine your temporary resting place until Christ returns to judge the living and the dead: **2Cor. 5:10**, "For we must all appear before the judgment seat of Christ, so that each one may receive what is due for what he has done in the body, whether good or evil."

You can deny God and live as if the world is the only thing you'll ever be accountable to, or you can embrace the love and mercy of the Creator through the redemptive blood of His only Son. The former guarantees you a place of torment until Christ returns, at which point you will be cast permanently into the lake of fire with your master, the devil; the latter will be more beautiful than you could ever imagine. **1Co. 2:9**, "But, as it is written, 'What no eye has seen, nor ear heard, nor the heart of man imagined, what God has prepared for those who love him.'"

The saddest thing is that most people who have the privilege of living their lives on this earth do so while ignoring the God who granted them that privilege. Unfortunately, heaven will have fewer souls than hell. **Mat. 7:13-14**,

> "Enter by the narrow gate. For the gate is wide and the way is easy that leads to destruction, and those who enter by it are many. For the gate is narrow and the way is hard that leads to life, and those who find it are few."

What will the secret message on your tombstone say?

Chapter 90
Encourage Future Preachers

"And he commanded us to preach to the people and to testify that he is the one appointed by God to be judge of the living and the dead" (**Act. 10:42**). Currently, we are training only half the required number of preachers needed for all the Churches of Christ in the United States. This is shocking for several reasons. It indicates challenging times ahead, as men from the congregation must step up and preach when no preachers are available. Some of these men are elders, deacons, or other mature members of the congregation, and they are sound in their faith. They are willing to preach and teach in the short term, but while they are capable, they do not wish to do so for an extended period. The longer it takes to find a preacher, the more challenging it becomes for these willing men to continue offering their valuable services.

Some well-intentioned men stand up and do their best, but because they lack maturity in the Word, they risk speaking things that are not in the Bible. Others take the opportunity to preach their interpretation of what they have read, intentionally promoting their ideas instead of biblical doctrine. This creates issues within the congregation, and before long, discord and unhappiness prevail. Over time, false doctrines are introduced, weakening the church and causing many to depart. Unfortunately, there are always some weaker Christians who can be led astray by these false teachers—individuals the Bible warns about in **Act. 20:19**.

> "I know that after my departure, fierce wolves will come in among you, not sparing the flock; and from among your own selves will arise men speaking twisted things, to draw away the disciples after them."

When a man stands at the pulpit, he is responsible for preaching the undefiled Word of God, free from his personal opinions or beliefs. Those who undertake that responsibility, whether as a calling or a volunteer, should remember the words of **1Pe. 4:11**: "Whoever speaks, as one who speaks the oracles of God." But why can't we find young men willing to step into the role of a minister anymore? What has led them to choose "normal" jobs over preaching? And why have so many preachers left the service of the Lord for secular employment? One reason, strangely enough, is the independent nature of the church. Yes, the very reason we are distinct from the denominations of the world is also why they no longer want to serve as preachers.

They assert that the autonomous structure permits the congregation or elders to decide at will whether a preacher should be dismissed, leading to an unstable and stressful job. Furthermore, most preachers do not receive medical benefits or 401(k) contributions from the church. Additionally, they do not earn enough to adequately prepare for retirement. Some have pointed out the church's conservative position as a reason for their hesitance to preach. They believe women should have a more significant role and feel that the absence of musical instruments and a praise team is discouraging and harmful to the church's growth.

It seems that the very principles by which we operate scripturally are cited as reasons for their willingness to leave the ministry or avoid it altogether. None of these issues are new. It's not as if preachers in the Church of Christ have ever received large salaries or benefit packages, so those reasons lack scriptural support. Christ has not changed, and neither has the Word. "Jesus Christ is the same yesterday, today, and forever" (**Heb. 13:8**). Another reason men hesitate to enter the ministry, and why some preachers leave it altogether, is the declining church. As more people are drawn away from the church, it becomes increasingly difficult for the church to support a preacher.

Even churches that could support preachers working in other areas struggle to maintain that support, making the prospect of becoming a preacher quite daunting. However, if no one is trained to preach, many churches will lack effective, doctrinally sound pulpit ministers and may be tempted to adopt more charismatic services. We must ensure that we encourage any young man considering a preaching career, and we should all take the time to thank those already preaching for their hard work.

Chapter 91
Becoming a More Effective Proclaimer

"Now a Jew named Apollos, a native of Alexandria, came to Ephesus. He was an eloquent man, competent in the Scriptures. He had been instructed in the way of the Lord. And being fervent in spirit, he spoke and taught accurately the things concerning Jesus, though he knew only the baptism of John. He began to speak boldly in the synagogue, but when Priscilla and Aquila heard him, they took him aside and explained the way of God more accurately.

And when he wished to cross to Achaia, the brothers encouraged him and wrote to the disciples to welcome him. When he arrived, he greatly helped those who through grace had believed, for he powerfully refuted the Jews in public, showing by the Scriptures that the Christ was Jesus" (**Act. 18:24-28**).

We all know Paul. He has been studied more than any other New Testament writer, and with good reason. After all, he was the "Apostle to the Gentiles." However, he was not the only remarkable Christian of his time. Today, we will examine Apollos, a contemporary of Paul who was highly skilled in preaching God's Word. The Bible tells us he was eloquent and competent, but then we read in verse 26 that something was lacking. Although he had been instructed in the way of the Lord, his teaching about Jesus was insufficient. Specifically, he was not preaching the Gospel, did not understand the significance of Jesus' death and resurrection, and therefore only preached John's baptism.

There are many preachers and teachers like Apollos in the world today. They are eloquent speakers, somewhat educated in the scriptures, and confidently bold about what they teach regarding the Bible. However, like Apollos, enthusiasm and a decent knowledge of the Bible are not enough. In the case of Paul's contemporary, it took two individuals sent from God to further educate him in the way of Jesus. I can imagine his surprise when Aquila and Priscilla took him aside to explain the "rest of the story" to him.

Two noteworthy aspects of our story today deserve mention. First, the two co-founders of the Corinthian church did not embarrass Apollos. They did not ambush him in front of everyone or criticize him for not sharing the complete truth. They recognized his enthusiasm but acknowledged his shortcomings and gently pulled him aside to address them. Many people would have called him out and shamed him, especially in today's climate, but Aquila and Priscilla did neither. They exhibited decency and respect by taking him aside to teach him. Second, he accepted their efforts graciously. When people feel compelled to correct us, even respectfully, we often become upset because our fragile feelings are hurt. Instead of listening and learning, we frequently become aggressively defensive, overlooking their well-intentioned efforts.

When our family and friends take the time to visit us, we should embody the spirit of Apollos by being grateful, appreciating their efforts, and striving to become more effective messengers of God's Word. Each of us has been like Apollos at some point in our spiritual journey. We have limited knowledge of the scriptures but are still eager to share the Good News. We confidently proclaim ideas that seem logical and doctrinally sound to us, even though they may not be so at all. The evident risk of excessive enthusiasm, combined with insufficient supporting facts, can inadvertently lead a seeking soul astray by providing them with false information.

However, if we are fortunate, we will have an Aquila and Priscilla in our lives, who care enough to gently guide us in the right direction. This will allow us to learn more about our God and Savior and instill in us the confidence to share the truth according to the scriptures rather than the opinions of man. Only then can we effectively counter those who oppose the Gospel of Christ. There is no doubt that we should share the Gospel with those who remain in darkness sin: **Mat. 28:19-20,**

> "Go therefore and make disciples of all nations, baptizing them in the name of the Father and of the Son and of the Holy Spirit, teaching them to observe all that I have commanded you. And behold, I am with you always, to the end of the age."

Since souls depend on our accurate teaching of the Word, we should take great care to ensure that we do so soundly. Similarly, Paul instructed his understudy, Titus, "But as for you, teach what accords with sound doctrine" (**Tit. 2:1**).

Chapter 92
The One Who "Shuts the Doors?"

"A son honors his father, and a servant his master. If then I am a father, where is my honor? And if I am a master, where is my fear? says the Lord of hosts to you, O priests, who despise my name. But you say, 'How have we despised your name?' By offering polluted food upon my altar. But you say, 'How have we polluted you?' By saying that the Lord's table may be despised. When you offer blind animals in sacrifice, is that not evil? And when you offer those that are lame or sick, is that not evil?

Present that to your governor; will he accept you or show you favor? says the Lord of hosts. And now entreat the favor of God, that he may be gracious to us. With such a gift from your hand, will he show favor to any of you? says the Lord of hosts. Oh that there were one among you who would shut the doors, that you might not kindle fire on my altar in vain! I have no pleasure in you, says the Lord of hosts, and I will not accept an offering from your hand" (**Mal. 6:1-10**).

Through the prophet Malachi, God confronts the priests of that time for offering blemished animals instead of what He commanded them to. **Deut. 15:21** makes it clear about the quality of the animal to be offered: "But if it has any blemish, if it is lame or blind or has any serious blemish, you shall not sacrifice it to the Lord your God." Only the very best from the flock could be offered to please God and temporarily atone for the sins the people had committed. The importance of offering an unblemished lamb is also reflected in the sacrifice of Jesus, **1Pe. 1:18-19** states,

> "knowing that you were ransomed from the futile ways inherited from your forefathers, not with perishable things such as silver or gold, but with the precious blood of Christ, like that of a lamb without blemish or spot."

Unfortunately, the perfect sacrifice was not offered in Malachi's time. When faced with their inadequate sacrifices, they reacted as people often do – showing shock, even disbelief, and asking a foolish question like, "How have we despised Your name?" Let me make this more personal for you with this question: "Will that be said of you on the Day of Judgment?" If you were to reflect on your current spiritual state, could that be said of you now? We must consistently offer our best to God, not only when it suits us or when we are seeking something, but also when we are sitting in church preparing to take communion.

We should always offer our very best to Him who created us from dust, **1Co. 10:31** states, "So, whether you eat or drink, or whatever you do, do all to the glory of God." There is never a time when our sacrifice to God should take a back seat to our earthly desires. How can we glorify our Creator if we do not give Him the very best we have? And no, we don't need to run into the field or go to our local farmers' market to find an unblemished lamb to sacrifice for our sins—that has been accomplished once and for all by Jesus. However, this does not mean our sacrifice to God is unnecessary. **Rom. 12:1** says,

> "I appeal to you therefore, brothers, by the mercies of God, to present your bodies as a living sacrifice, holy and acceptable to God, which is your spiritual worship."

You are the living sacrifice. Everything you do should be for the glory of God, and all of it should be as unblemished as possible. The only way to achieve that is to rid your body of old desires, put on a new self, and be "transformed by the renewal of your mind..." God did not accept second best in the time of Malachi, and He will not accept it now either. Grace may cover a multitude of sins, but it does not mean you can intentionally offer damaged goods to the God who gave you life and provided salvation through His perfect Son.

Consider this the next time you give less than you can when you sing those psalms, look at your phone during communion, ignore the needs of those you could help, or treat sleep or a football game as more important than Sunday worship. Reflect on how you blaspheme His Holy name by using "Om." as a catch-all term, and recognize when your actions reflect poorly on Him. Instead, strive to be the person God describes who would "shut the doors so that you might not kindle fire on His altar in vain!" In other words, give Him your very best so that you can be confident in His promise of eternal life in heaven one day.

Chapter 93
What Will Your Response Be?

There is generally one of three responses individuals give to God's calling for their lives. The first one is rejection. **Jon. 1:1-2,**

> "Now the word of the Lord came to Jonah the son of Amittai, saying, 'Arise, go to Nineveh, that great city, and call out against it, for their evil has come up before me.'"

God was calling Jonah to speak on His behalf to the people of Nineveh, but he chose to run away instead of obediently following God's direction. He did not want to engage with the people God was sending him to. **Jon. 1:3,**

> "But Jonah rose to flee to Tarshish from the presence of the Lord. He went down to Joppa and found a ship going to Tarshish. So he paid the fare and went down into it, to go with them to Tarshish, away from the presence of the Lord."

That kind of response is not unusual today, either. God places a mission on someone's heart, and they reject it. They attempt to pursue a calling of their choosing, believing that the omnipresent God cannot find them. Of course, this doesn't necessarily involve physical running or a specific location, but instead exists in their minds. Their act of rejection serves as a way to ignore God, hiding from Him by pretending they don't hear Him or that they are too busy to listen.

The second type of response is objection. **Exo. 3:10**, "Come, I will send you to Pharaoh that you may bring my people, the children of Israel, out of Egypt." It was a somewhat more complex calling than Jonah's, but it still had the might of the Lord behind it. Moses had four objections **Exo. 3:11**, "But Moses said to God, 'Who am I that I should go to Pharaoh and bring the children of Israel out of Egypt?'" **Exo. 3:13**, "...If I come to the people of Israel and say to them, 'The God of your fathers has sent me to you,' and they ask me, 'What is his name?' what shall I say to them?'" **Exo. 4:1**, "...But behold, they will not believe me or listen to my voice, for they will say, 'The Lord did not appear to you.'" **Exo. 4:10**, "Oh, my Lord, I am not eloquent, either in the past or since you have spoken to your servant, but I am slow of speech and of tongue." People often make excuses to disqualify themselves from God's calling, as if God has overlooked their shortcomings and would suddenly say, "Oops! You are right, my child. Let Me find someone else to do My bidding."

The third response is acceptance. **Gen. 12:1** states, "Now the Lord said to Abram, 'Go from your country and your kindred and your father's house to the land that I will show you.'" Jonah was called to a specific city and rejected the call, while Moses' calling was more complex yet still specific in nature, and he objected. In contrast to the first two, Abraham's calling was non-specific. It resembled a message to "Take your family and start traveling, and when you reach the place I am sending you, I will tell you to stop." How intimidating is that? And yet, every day, Christians around the world do just that. They figuratively (or literally) pack their belongings and venture into the unknown towards an uncertain future, but with the assurance that with God, nothing is impossible.

When Jesus discussed the difficulty for a rich man to enter heaven, His disciples posed a legitimate question: "...Who then can be saved?" (**Mat. 19:25**). Jesus replied, "...With man this is impossible, but with God all things are possible" (**Mat. 19:26**). Those who hear God's calling and do not hesitate to follow it possess a unique understanding of this verse, along with **Php. 4:13**, "I can do all things through Him who strengthens me." This does not imply a lack of trepidation; instead, their reliance on and faith in God is so strong that they act despite their fears. He found Jonah; you cannot run and hide. He answered Moses; you cannot effectively make excuses.

It would be best for you to step out in faith and follow His will for your life. Regardless, God will get your attention, and although you may resist or object initially, great success awaits you if you ultimately listen. Jonah saved a city, Moses led a nation out of captivity, delivered the Ten Commandments, and brought them to the borders of the Promised Land. To Abram, this promise was made: **Gen. 12:2-3**,

"And I will make of you a great nation, and I will bless you and make your name great, so that you will be a blessing. I will bless those who bless you, and him who dishonors you I will curse, and in you all the families of the earth shall be blessed."

God may not always call you to build an ark, leave your country, lead people out of captivity, fight a giant, warn a city, or proclaim His word to generation after generation like the Apostle Paul. He might simply call you to minister to those you meet, teach a Bible class, engage in local outreach, help the needy, or assist with church activities. But don't be mistaken—every obedient "callee" is a vital part of the spiritual salvation wheel of God's mighty and glorious kingdom. So, when He calls you, how will you respond?

Chapter 94
From God's Word, Not Man's Books

"And I applied my heart to seek and to search out by wisdom all that is done under heaven. It is an unhappy business that God has given to the children of man to be busy with. I have seen everything that is done under the sun, and behold, all is vanity and a striving after wind. What is crooked cannot be made straight, and what is lacking cannot be counted.

I said in my heart, "I have acquired great wisdom, surpassing all who were over Jerusalem before me, and my heart has had great experience of wisdom and knowledge." And I applied my heart to know wisdom and to know madness and folly. I perceived that this also is but a striving after wind. For in much wisdom is much vexation, and he who increases knowledge increases sorrow" (**Ecc. 1:13-18**).

By all historical accounts, King Solomon, the author of Ecclesiastes, was well known for his wealth, wisdom, and writings. The king, the second after David and the last ruler of a unified kingdom, wrote these words to criticize earthly wisdom, not because it lacks value, but as a warning. You might rightfully ask, "Why the warning? Isn't wisdom something the Bible specifically encourages us to pursue?" The answer is "Yes." **Pro. 8:11** calls it precious: "for wisdom is better than jewels, and all that you may desire cannot compare with her." Through symbolic language, the author emphasizes its qualities in the following verse: "I, wisdom, dwell with prudence, and I find knowledge and discretion." And that is not the only instance. In **Pro. 3:13-18**, it is compared to a fine woman,

> "Blessed is the one who finds wisdom, and the one who gets understanding, for the gain from her is better than gain from silver and her profit better than gold. She is more precious than jewels, and nothing you desire can compare with her. Long life is

in her right hand; in her left hand are riches and honor. Her ways are ways of pleasantness, and all her paths are peace. She is a tree of life to those who lay hold of her; those who hold her fast are called blessed."

Even the New Testament emphasizes the importance of gaining wisdom, informing the reader that God will not deny it to those who seek its treasures: **Jam. 1:5**, "If any of you lacks wisdom, let him ask God, who gives generously to all without reproach, and it will be given him." Clearly, the Bible views wisdom as a crucial aspect of successful living. So, what does Solomon have against it? His point is that our primary goal in studying should be to enhance our spiritual wisdom first, as this will keep our lives centered on God rather than earthly motivations like titles and accolades. However, to understand wisdom, we need to recognize the essential differences between it and its close relative, knowledge. The latter does not necessarily encompass the former, but the former always includes it.

Knowledge reflects the clarity gained through diligent study. In contrast, wisdom arises from practical experience and involves the ability to thoughtfully and effectively apply acquired knowledge to make sound, discerning decisions. In other words, you may excel in academic knowledge yet struggle to find meaningful ways to apply it in real life. Indeed, with extensive knowledge, the world may bestow upon you numerous accolades and trophies, even naming buildings, streets, and other entities in your honor. Nonetheless, if that wisdom isn't rooted in God, it ultimately ends with you. While the building may stand long after your passing, and the world might remember you for centuries as it does Aristotle and Da Vinci, chapters and books may also be written in your memory. However, what benefit does that provide you after you're gone?

What benefit would that bring you in the afterlife? I would expect quite the opposite of what you seek. However, if you were unwise in worldly matters yet wise in spiritual ones, you would possess the wisdom to remain obedient to God's word, and your death would signify the beginning of a beautiful future. Furthermore, if you pursued knowledge and wisdom in the Bible rather than solely from the world, you could echo the words of Paul in **1Co. 2:13**, "And we impart this in words not taught by human wisdom but taught by the Spirit, interpreting spiritual truths to those who are spiritual." Recognize where true wisdom resides – in God's Word, not man's books. Acknowledge the true teacher of wisdom– God's Spirit, not man.

Chapter 95
Step Out of the City

> "For the bodies of those animals whose blood is brought into the holy places by the high priest as a sacrifice for sin are burned outside the camp. So, Jesus also suffered outside the gate in order to sanctify the people through his own blood. Therefore, let us go to him outside the camp and bear the reproach he endured. For here we have no lasting city, but we seek the city that is to come" (**Heb. 13:11-14**).

After a spotless animal was sacrificed on the Day of Atonement, the remainder was ordered to be burned outside the camp. **Exo. 29:14** states, "But the flesh of the bull and its skin and its dung you shall burn with fire outside the camp; it is a sin offering."

This occurred in a ceremonially clean location, and even the priest who performed the burning needed to be cleansed before returning. It might seem odd to do so. **Lev. 16:28** states, "And he who burns them shall wash his clothes and bathe his body in water, and afterward he may come into the camp." The obvious question this commandment raises is, "Why not just eat what is left instead of wasting what remains of the carcass?" Since it had been used in a sin offering for all the people of Israel, it was deemed unclean and unsuitable for consumption by the purified people of God. It's important to note that the animal could be eaten for many other sacrifices aside from the designated Day of Atonement.

Joh. 19:20 states, "Many of the Jews read this inscription, for the place where Jesus was crucified was near the city, and it was written in Aramaic, Latin, and Greek." The author emphasizes an otherwise obscure point: "Just as the animal that bore the sins of the people was taken outside the camp, Jesus, who bore the sins of all people by his blood, suffered outside the gate." What a figuratively rich comparison this is—one that could be explored in depth by those who find it intriguing. However, I want to draw our attention to the next part of today's text, **vs. 13-14**. What is suggested here is important for every Christian who faithfully follows Jesus. Just as your Savior suffered and died for you to make you holy and acceptable to God, you should be ready to go 'outside' your camp and suffer for Him.

At the time Hebrews was written, Christians faced significant persecution, and they may not have wanted to venture into the streets of Jerusalem. To make matters worse, the heinous actions of Emperor Nero, who made Christians scapegoats for the burning of part of Rome, must have been fresh in their minds. Who could truly blame them for being afraid, given what they were enduring? However, the author wanted his readers to overcome their fear and hesitation. This same lesson applies to us today. We must be courageous in our spiritual walk and face the dangers without fear since we know two things. First, our persecution is guaranteed, **Joh. 15:18-20**,

> "If the world hates you, know that it has hated me before it hated you. If you were of the world, the world would love you as its own; but because you are not of the world, but I chose you out of the world, therefore the world hates you. Remember the word that I said to you: 'A servant is not greater than his master.' If they persecuted me, they will also persecute you."

Secondly, the Creator God is on our side, and we have the armor to defend against and overcome those persecutions (**Eph. 6:10-18**). We overcome by meeting Christ and walking with Him, and the only place to do that is outside the city. In other words, society will cast us aside, and we will undoubtedly need to step out of our comfort zone. We should go to the place where He was crucified to properly meet our Savior—away from the glitz and glamour of the world. Our fear should never be of persecution by man or even losing our standing and status in society for putting Christ on in baptism.

This is because our earthly dwelling is temporary; our true dwelling awaits us in heaven, where we will spend a blissful eternity with the Father. If Jesus was willing to go outside the gates to be crucified for our salvation, we should be prepared to step outside the gate to meet Him. Furthermore, as I mentioned earlier, being outside the gate is beyond our comfort zone.

Leaving the city demonstrates a willingness to sacrifice worldly things for the spiritual. That is where we will find opportunities to reach out to those still in darkness, to witness to the waiter or the mechanic fixing our car. That is where we will encounter the abused spouse, the hurting child, the discontented, the anguished, and the seekers.

If we remain within the city, surrounded by its many lavish distractions, we will not be effective ambassadors for the peace that comes from the hope we find in Christ. Therefore, step outside the city, meet Christ in person, engage in the good fight, and proclaim the gospel.

Chapter 96
She Is More Than I Deserve

"He who finds a wife finds a good thing and obtains favor from the Lord" (**Pro. 18:22**). Today, my wife and I will celebrate 25 years of marriage. I was "naughty" in my younger days and was not the man I would want my sons to be. I was self-centered and disloyal in my relationships. Moreover, I was a non-practicing Catholic (whatever that means), so I never set foot inside a church—not even for those "special" holidays. Consequently, I had no Christian influence in my life. I attended weddings and funerals but never listened to a word the preacher said. Unfortunately, I smoked, cursed, and indulged in worldly desires. As I mentioned, I am not proud of who I was.

But I changed. I met the woman of my dreams in my mid-thirties and married her three years later. Because of her, I started attending church and decided to be someone my daughter, whom I was about to adopt, would be proud of. I couldn't change my past, but I could change my future – and so I did. I believe my wife and I have a unique relationship. I'm not saying that no other couples share a similar bond, but I will confidently assert that few do. From day one, we have spent most of our time together. One might think being together day in and day out would be frustrating, but it is not.

Here's the part that most people believe we are faking or outright lying about. In those 25 years, we have never once fought. We have never said anything disparaging, never threatened, never acted aggressively, never cursed, and never thrown anything at each other...ever. We neither storm out in anger nor give each other the silent treatment. We have disagreements but never let them spiral out of control, and we always resolve them quickly. In other words, when we disagree, we do so respectfully and find a solution together.

Every morning, we wake up excited to be next to each other. We say "I love you" countless times a day, and we laugh a lot—really, a lot. We encourage each other whenever we can and have each other's backs. When we sit beside each other, we always hold hands. Every time we kiss, we do so three times, once for each of our children. We might annoy some friends because we've never gone through a "rough patch." None of this is a lie; what you see at church or during our visits is what happens at home. In fact, at home, it's even better. People tell us it's unhealthy never to fight. No, it isn't. It may be unhealthy never to disagree, but it's not unhealthy to be happy.

The question of how we can maintain such a strong relationship has been asked of us on multiple occasions. This is my response. First, we are a God-fearing couple. We may love each other, but we love God first. Every morning, we pray individually, and every evening, we pray together, thanking Him for our love. I don't believe I deserve someone as wonderful as her, and she does not believe she deserves me. God placed her in my life to transform me, and I have changed. Women are treasures given to us by the Creator, and we should treat them with great respect. We ought to protect them, shower them with love, and thank God daily for them, both in word and action. But above all, we should treat them as our Heavenly Father expects us.

As a counselor, I have witnessed too many unhappy relationships, and I promised God I would never put her through anything like that. We have faced tough times (not because of each other) and have overcome them together. Those difficulties, and there have been many, have only deepened our love for each other. I will never be who I once was again, and I have a daughter, a son-in-law, two sons, two granddaughters, and friends to set an example for. They will see what a happily ever after should look like: not perfect, not without the challenges life throws at it, but a team that is respectful, loyal, honorable, and loving to one another.

They will witness what implicit trust looks like, what sincere dedication embodies, and what a Christian married couple represents. It requires hard work; I promise you that. You must always put in the effort, but it is so worth it. I will not waste a second of our fleeting time together on this earth by making her unhappy. She deserves more than I can provide, and I will spend every moment until my dying breath striving to be the man worthy of her love. She is more than my wife, more than my best friend; she is my soulmate.

Chapter 97
Courage Under Fire

"Then the king of Egypt said to the Hebrew midwives, one of whom was named Shiphrah and the other Puah, 'When you serve as midwife to the Hebrew women and see them on the birthstool, if it is a son, you shall kill him, but if it is a daughter, she shall live'" (**Exo. 1:15-16**).

After the death of Joseph and his brothers, a new pharaoh rose to power, but he was unaware of the Hebrew patriarch. His primary concern at that time was the increasing population of the Israelites. Fearing that they would continue to multiply and potentially align with Egypt's enemies, he devised what he likely believed was a clever plan.

> **Exo. 1:9-11**, "And he said to his people, 'Behold, the people of Israel are too many and too mighty for us. Come, let us deal shrewdly with them, lest they multiply, and, if war breaks out, they join our enemies and fight against us and escape from the land.' Therefore, they set taskmasters over them to afflict them with heavy burdens."

The plan was to weaken the nation, but it failed miserably, compelling the king to devise another, more sinister scheme. He ordered the Hebrew midwives to kill the male infants at birth. The midwives' response to the Pharaoh's plan is recorded in **Exo. 1:17**, "But the midwives feared God and did not do as the king of Egypt commanded them, but let the male children live."

The midwives, tasked with carrying out Pharaoh's brutal decree to kill the newborn Hebrew boys as a means of controlling the Israelite population, courageously refused to comply, choosing instead to honor God and protect innocent lives. Their reverent fear of God and unwavering allegiance to Him gave them the courage to defy Pharaoh's command to harm the male infants. Can you imagine the dire consequences of defying a despotic Egyptian ruler?

Torture or even death would have been almost certain, yet these midwives showed remarkable bravery in the face of overwhelming danger.

There is much for us to learn from that story. Their courage set the stage for another tale that would soon unfold: a Hebrew boy would be born, hidden in plain sight, and then raised as an Egyptian. After some time, he would lead God's people out of captivity and to the doorway of the promised land. Had they complied with the order to murder the male babies, Moses would almost certainly have been one of the victims, and there would have been no Exodus story. Would you display such courage when faced with a similar situation? Or do you think that could never happen to you? After all, you are not a midwife. You are not one, but that does not mean you wouldn't encounter something similar.

Let me explain with an analogy. The midwives were ordered to kill the Hebrew babies, and the pharaoh-king of this world is making the same demand. Just as those women were present at the birth, you and I will also be present at the delivery – the second birth of a baptized believer. Your role as a midwife would involve studying God's Word with that person, nurturing them, and watching them grow from an embryonic seeker to a newborn baby in Christ. So, you would be there at their birth, so to speak. And you should not be afraid: **Isa 41:10,**

> "fear not, for I am with you; be not dismayed, for I am your God;
> I will strengthen you, I will help you, I will uphold you with my righteous right hand."

The devil desires their death because he does not want God's kingdom to grow, so he tries to influence us to figuratively slaughter them. We accomplish this by neglecting their growth after baptism and idly standing by as they suffer from spiritual starvation, ultimately returning to the world and the impending doom that awaits them. Do you have the courage to say, "No, not me! I will not allow that. My faith in and fear of God is greater than any fear I have of the devil and man." If you choose courage over fear, there is good news for you. God will reward you abundantly for your loyalty. I know this to be true because God blessed the midwives: **Exo. 1:21,** "And because the midwives feared God, he gave them families."

Chapter 98
Clarity From a Missing Verse

"And as they were going along the road they came to some water, and the eunuch said, 'See, here is water! What prevents me from being baptized?'" [37](missing) [38.] And he commanded the chariot to stop, and they both went down into the water, Philip and the eunuch, and he baptized him" (**Act. 8:36-38**). KJV.

Except for the King James translation of the Bible, most others omit **v. 37**, "And Philip said, If thou believest with all thine heart, thou mayest. And he answered and said, I believe that Jesus Christ is the Son of God." Why would one translation include it while others do not? The answer is both simple and intriguing. The reason for the omission is that the oldest manuscripts do not include it.

Many people are unaware that numerous manuscripts exist. In fact, I know experienced Christians who do not realize that there are manuscripts from which the words of the modern Bible are derived. Few Bible classes have addressed this specifically, so casual students might assume that the first Bible was the KJV. I don't have the space in this article to list all the names, but it's enough to say that there are more than 24970 manuscripts or parts of them. Yes, that is an overwhelming number, but it also attests to the authenticity of the Bible. So why is the omission of a single verse intriguing? Let's reread it before I share my thoughts on the matter.

"And Philip said, If thou believest with all thine heart, thou mayest. And he answered and said, I believe that Jesus Christ is the Son of God." Let's begin at the beginning and work our way forward. Philip is directed by the Angel of the Lord to "Rise and go south...to the desert place..." Without hesitation, the obedient servant of God makes his way to the road "...that goes down from Jerusalem to Gaza." There, he meets a eunuch returning from worshipping in Jerusalem, and together, they study the words of the prophet Isaiah and the story of Jesus. They reach a body of water at some point, and the eunuch utters the famous words, "See, here is water! What prevents me from being baptized."

The Church of Christ regards these words as a testimony to the validity of baptism. Meanwhile, some denominations assert that it is simply a hasty sign of the eunuch identifying with Philip's teachings. These two viewpoints have been vigorously debated for centuries, and I am certain that my thoughts will not lead to a resolution, but here they are nonetheless. The eagerness to be baptized without including **v. 37** could be argued endlessly, but clarity emerges when the missing verse is added. I won't advocate for its inclusion, but since the early church fathers considered it significant, it must have special meaning, at the very least.

Those later manuscripts seem to have included the words to emphasize baptism, not merely as an outward sign of inward grace but as something far more significant. The argument that there was a sudden urge to identify with the teacher or a general acceptance of the teachings seems particularly weak when **v. 37** is included. Those who argue for that view cite Simon the Sorcerer in **Act. 8:13**, but this specifically refers to someone who lacked understanding of the message and believed he could purchase its benefits. Furthermore, why would there be such an instance of urging, emphasized by the solemnity of the words in **v. 37**, if all it required was the baptism of the Holy Spirit?

And while we're on that point, Simon did not ask for an immersive baptism but rather for a laying on of hands, which does not support their claim. Why they were allowed to pass on the Holy Spirit by laying on hands is a topic for another time, but **Act. 2:38** makes it clear when we receive the Holy Spirit:

> "And Peter said to them, 'Repent and be baptized every one of you in the name of Jesus Christ for the forgiveness of your sins, and you will receive the gift of the Holy Spirit.'"

We could also explore the term "baptism," which means "immersion," but that discussion is for another time. This article serves solely as a reflection on my thoughts regarding **v. 37** and its contribution to understanding the Eunuch's story.

Chapter 99
The Challenge to Dig Deeper

"The saying is trustworthy, for: If we have died with him, we will also live with him; if we endure, we will also reign with him; if we deny him, he also will deny us; if we are faithless, he remains faithful— for he cannot deny himself" (**2Ti. 2:11-13**).

These scriptures are not obscure; you've likely heard them recited in sermons, Bible classes, or as evidence in arguments. I love these verses because they challenge me to dig deeper each time I encounter them. While each verse could warrant an entire article, here's a brief overview of today's passages.

I smile at the first four words used to emphasize the subsequent statements. This is because, by definition, all of the Bible's words are trustworthy. Naturally, this perspective is shaped by hindsight; the original audience lacked access to the 66 books of the Bible that we have today. I often wonder how they might have reacted if they had possessed it. Would they have engaged in the same debates we do, deciding what to accept as trustworthy and what to discard? While they wrestled with these challenges, they at least had the excuse of not having the complete Biblical text.

We are fortunate to have **2Ti. 3:16**, which asserts, "All Scripture is breathed out by God." However, even this assurance does not eliminate all questions. One that arises for me is, "When do we die with Him?" Paul indicates a specific moment in time, as death itself is not a gradual process; it arrives suddenly-when the last breath leaves your lungs. **Rom. 6:4a** clarifies this timing: "We were buried therefore with Him by baptism into death." According to this scripture, our death occurs "by baptism into death." While one could argue this point, I view it as more than a mere reference to the practice of baptism by immersion.

It also promises that we will live with Him, as highlighted in **Rom. 6:4b**, "...in order that, just as Christ was raised from the dead by the glory of the Father, we too might walk in newness of life." The blood of Christ purchased this new life, and through obedience, it embodies "the assurance of things hoped for, the conviction of things not seen" (**Heb. 11:1**). The phrase "If we endure" becomes the fulcrum of our obedience. To endure is to face and overcome the trials and tragedies of the Christian journey. We have a choice: we can either strive to "reign with Him" or succumb to sin and its eternal consequences.

I would be remiss not to reference **Jam. 1:12**, "Blessed is the man who remains steadfast under trial, for when he has stood the test he will receive the crown of life, which God has promised to those who love him." In Jesus' message to the seven churches in Revelation, He addresses the conquerors who will reign with Him. For the purpose of this article, I will cite **Rev. 3:21**: "The one who conquers, I will grant him to sit with me on my throne, as I also conquered and sat down with my Father on his throne."

Will a faithful, just, and fair Christ acknowledge us if we deny Him? Of course, He will not. **Mat. 10:32-33** states,

> "So everyone who acknowledges me before men, I also will acknowledge before my Father who is in heaven, but whoever denies me before men, I also will deny before my Father who is in heaven."

We have a choice: we can play silly games and win trivial prizes, or we can play for eternal life, the ultimate reward. Jesus will not intercede on behalf of those who live as "pretend Christians." Can we really believe we can fool Him by merely checking the attendance card on a Sunday while living like the world the rest of the week? We may deceive man, but we cannot deceive God. Denying Him in this way leads to a sure discovery of the alternatives to heaven. The beauty of these verses lies in the stark reminder that, even when we falter, we serve a God who remains faithful despite our shortcomings.

His faithfulness shines through our struggles, especially as we move from the darkness of sin to the glorious light of salvation. Even when we were lost and persecuting the church, denigrating His Holy Name, God patiently waited for us to change direction. This faithfulness is beautifully encapsulated in **Rom. 5:8**: "…but God shows his love for us in that while we were still sinners, Christ died for us."

Chapter 100
There Is Strength in Numbers

"But exhort one another every day, as long as it is called 'today,' that none of you may be hardened by the deceitfulness of sin" (**Heb. 3:13**). No one who has lived for any length of time will disagree that life is challenging. Before we become Christians, we find ourselves entrenched in the darkness of sin, and we are not prime targets for the devil. Why would he see us as worthy adversaries if we are doing his bidding? Jesus' sharp remarks to the Jews who sought to harm Him clearly illustrate where the ultimate loyalty lies for some lie: **Joh. 8:44**, "You are of your father the devil, and your will is to do your father's desires."

On the other hand, those of us who willingly devote ourselves to obedient faithfulness to the Father through His Son, Jesus Christ, will undoubtedly be targets of the devil. And there is no escape from that reality: **Joh. 15:20**, "Remember the word that I said to you: 'A servant is not greater than his master.' If they persecuted Me, they will also persecute you..." It is as sure that we will face challenges as it is that the sun shone today, and unless Jesus returns to judge the living and the dead, it will shine again tomorrow. The evil one is cunning and will exploit our greatest weakness, baiting us like the proverbial carrot dangled in front of a donkey. He will watch eagerly as we stumble while trying to chase what distances us from God's love embrace.

It is certainly not impossible to overcome our sinful nature on our own, but doing so leaves us vulnerable to attacks we may not see coming. The devil does not always dangle a carrot; sometimes, he slyly introduces sinful practices into our lives through much subtler means. He can use the constant influence of music, movies, or video games to gradually wear down our defenses over time. Our resolve not to indulge in wrongdoing or support those who do may weaken, and before long, our Christianity becomes a mere speck in the rearview mirror of life. As mentioned, whether we actively participate in sin or not still places the consequences at our feet: **Rom. 1:32**, "Though they know God's righteous decree that those who practice such things deserve to die, they not only do them but give approval to those who practice them."

Here's something worth remembering today: "The easiest participatory medal to win is in the game of silence when sin abounds around us." While trying to defeat the cunning ways of the father of all lies is possible, it can also be perilous. However, there's an easier way for someone to stand up to the devil. I remember an army sergeant drilling this saying into our heads as recruits: "There is strength in numbers." It's easy to break a single matchstick, but have you ever tried breaking 25 at once? All it takes is for us to do something relatively simple, as we are told in today's scripture—exhort one another.

The Bible is filled with scriptures about encouragement. We see a similar sentiment in **1Th. 5:11**, "Therefore encourage one another and build one another up, just as you are doing." While Christianity is a personal decision that leads to an individual relationship with Christ, we were never meant to be alone or to fight the good fight by ourselves. We may be individuals, but we find our ultimate strength in the bond of Christian fellowship. **Heb. 10:25** states, "...not neglecting to meet together, as is the habit of some, but encouraging one another, and all the more as you see the Day drawing near." What a great reason to attend a local church.

Sometimes, we cannot see the forest for the tree before us. I write these articles almost daily, and now and then, I make a mistake. I may read them repeatedly, but my mind automatically corrects an obvious, glaring error, and I post the article. Kind brothers and sisters then reply to inform me of the mistake, and I correct it. I fail to see what is right in front of me. Sometimes, we also need encouragement to stay on the straight and narrow path. Their continuous encouragement instills in us a steadfast strength that steers us away from the perilous path we are on. Without their words, we might become "hardened by the deceitfulness of sin."

Their support may have a significant impact, regardless of how far we have wandered from the path of righteousness. **Jam. 5:19-20** says, "My brothers, if anyone among you strays from the truth and someone brings him back, let him know that whoever brings back a sinner from his wandering will save his soul from death and will cover a multitude of sins." Encourage someone today: it might change their "forever."

For the Butterfly and Unicorn Princesses

www.ingramcontent.com/pod-product-compliance
Lightning Source LLC
Chambersburg PA
CBHW031639040426
42453CB00006B/147